Country Home®
Collection

MEREDITH® BOOKS

Country Home.

Editor in Chief: Jean LemMon
Executive Editor: Ann Omvig Maine
Art Director: Peggy A. Fisher

Senior Editor: Beverly Hawkins
Copy Chief/Production Editor: Angela K. Renkoski
Interior Design Director: Candace Ord Manroe
Interior Designer: Joseph Boehm
Building Editor: Steve Cooper
Food and Tabletop Editor: Lisa Kingsley
Antiques and Garden Editor: Linda Joan Smith
Assistant Art Directors: Sue Mattes, Shelley Caldwell
Administrative Assistant: Becky A. Brame
Art Business Clerk: Jacalyn M. Mason
Editorial Trainee: Lisa C. Jones

President/Magazine Group: William T. Kerr

MEREDITH® BOOKS
President, Book Group: Joseph J. Ward
Vice President and Editorial Director: Elizabeth P. Rice
Executive Editor: Connie Schrader
Art Director: Ernest Shelton

COUNTRY HOME® COLLECTION
Editor: Jean LemMon
Project Editor: Marsha Jahns
Graphic Designer: Harijs Priekulis
Electronic Text Processor: Paula Forest

Contents

Deep within each of us is a nesting instinct—an urge to turn a house into a home. On these pages you'll see country "nesters" in newly

constructed houses, historic Cape Cods and saltboxes, carefree cottages, even a '50s ranch house. And while the structures are very different, all of these homes exude the same appealing warmth.

As any nester knows, that warmth is created by the little things—those personal touches that speak of our families and traditions, our connectedness with the past. It's no wonder, then, that the "nests" in this COUNTRY HOME® COLLECTION are some of the best we've seen.

Jean Lemmon

February

PASSION
IN PRACTICE

*Marcia and Bill Finks'
love of folk art doesn't
stop with collecting.
Painted metal folk
sculptures and rustic
furniture they make
themselves join collected
pieces in their Fenton,
Michigan, saltbox.*

BY CANDACE ORD MANROE

Far right: *Not just the early-style fireplace brings warmth to Marcia and Bill's family room. So do their limited-edition Uncle Sam and American Indian sculptures, which hold court in front of the hearth. The Finkses appreciate works by other folk artists. Flanking their mantel mirror is a cardboard horse by Navajo folk artist Mamie Deschillie, and on the window table is a carving by Sharon Pierce. The circa-1720 blanket chest is from Pennsylvania and features its original paint and handwrought hinges.*

Above right: *An American Indian-inspired twig-and-metal chair made by Bill helps define a corner of the family room where more folk art—log homes by contemporary folk artist Dean Johnson and a 19th-century game board—find a happy resting place.*

Nearly up to its eaves in snow, set back behind rustic wood fence rails, the saltbox home of Marcia and Bill Finks conjures up lonely images of 17th-century Massachusetts.

Isolation looms above the brittle, brown stalks of summer's residue that stand sentinel over a patch of melting snow. It is an isolation that makes nonsense of reality—of the fact that, scattered a neighborly distance apart, are several other homes.

That's only the start of the trickery. The Finkses' home isn't historic; it's barely three years old. Also, it's in the northern neck of the Midwest, not in New England.

Come spring and summer, the home will elude typecasting anew, shedding its forlorn winter skin, with its old New England texture, for a vibrant new life that smacks of the sunny south of France. Garlanded in flowers and herbs, the home will appear scooped straight out of the Provençal countryside.

Inside, a kindred unpredictability pervades. The home is a melange of the things its owners love best—old and new folk art and country furniture, along with offbeat odds and ends—the presence of which is justified solely by their appeal to the owners, not by any conformation to a period or style.

"Spontaneity is what we're striving for in everything these days," says Marcia.

PASSION
IN PRACTICE

Far left: *The living room, with its 19th-century folk art portrait, camelback sofa, and wing chairs, has a more formal air than any other space in the home. But even here, the humor of the unexpected infiltrates. A rustic coffee table made by Bill bears Marcia's American flag paintwork; a tall ladder, also made by Bill, leads nowhere.*

Left: *The owners' artistic eyes transform even a small kitchen into a series of inviting settings whose charms come from the clever mix of disparate elements, from old stoneware to a stuffed chicken.*

Below: *An elongated-back Finks-made chair echoes the architecture of the stairway that leads to the bedroom.*

"Five years ago," Bill says, "if we had owned this home it would've looked exactly the way it was *supposed* to, following all the rules for this kind of architecture."

Marcia adds, "It would've been completely country, down to sage green walls, to please other people—to fit what we thought was expected and appropriate."

But five years ago, Marcia and Bill were different people, more aligned with the status quo, more concerned about what others think.

Today, by self-admission, they are anything but typical nine-to-fivers. When circumstances precipitated a change in how they would earn a living, Marcia and Bill didn't waste time staring down their gift horse of opportunity. Instead, they quickly seized an alternate work style, making a career of the metal folk art and twig furniture that had started as a hobby.

"Bill had been in retail twenty-one years, then lost his job. When thinking about what to do next, we knew we didn't want conventional jobs, but something creative. Bill had made twig furniture to supplement our income while I was in school, so we decided to try that full time," says Marcia.

That was in February of 1990. In the scant two years since, Marcia and Bill have steered away from crafting twig furniture, devoting their time instead to making

PASSION
IN PRACTICE

their own brand of folk art using metal, wire, and paint. Bill cuts the metal and wire to form the piece, and Marcia adds her flourishes with paint.

Their offerings include tall, three-dimensional sculptures of metal American Indians and Uncle Sams; cutout, freestanding metal American Indians that look two-dimensional; and African- and Southwestern-inspired wall art and painted metal mirrors. (Major works are limited editions; less complex designs are not, but they're handmade and unique.)

"The truth is, we didn't take the time to analyze or plan," says Marcia. "This felt like the right thing to do, and we just jumped in."

"After all those years of profit sharing, insurance—we took the plunge just like that," says Bill, snapping his fingers.

Acting spontaneously, following their instincts more than their intellects, has worked. Not only are Marcia and Bill finally fulfilling their artistic impulses, they're receiving recognition. They are represented by one of the most respected folk art galleries in the country—Jay Johnson, Inc., America's Folk Heritage Gallery in New York City. Their pieces also have been marketed in the gift shops of the Museum of American Folk Art in New York City.

Plus, the couple participated in a folk art show at the Very Special Arts Gallery in Washington, D.C., and another at the Pelham Art Center in New York.

"We've been amazed at the response," says Bill. They no longer fear indifference to their work at the various crafts fairs in which they participate across the country. These

Left: *A majority of the finish work on their folk art is completed by the Finkses in their dining room, which features an unlikely blend of antiques, art, and accessories, including a 19th-century folk portrait, oddball carved wooden heads, and bird nests.*
Above: *Decorating to please themselves, the Finkses top a dining room piesafe with the sculptural forms of a salvaged finial and a broken carving.*

PASSION
IN PRACTICE

days, it seems everyone wants their art; now they fear having time to create.

But somehow they find a way, even if it means working long nights.

One reason the Finkses are able to keep up their energy is because they work at home—at their own pace, in their own style of clothes (blue jeans, usually—and possibly both with hair pulled back in ponytails), and to their own special drummer (when they feel creative, they work; when they don't, they *don't*).

"Our home feels good to us, and I'm sure that working here inspires creativity and energizes us," says Marcia.

And well it should. The Finkses' home is a study in creativity. The same spontaneity that launched their folk art careers informs their home.

The dining room where Marcia paints includes a 19th-century folk portrait on the wall—and carved, almost macabre folk heads in a startlingly different style on an antique cupboard. Bird nests join antique pottery; an old finial, long lost from its original host, stands like sculpture on a piesafe.

And the entire home is invigorated by the folk art and furniture, including flag-painted rustic tables, made by Marcia and Bill.

"Now, we just put things in our home that make us feel good and trust that it'll all fall into place," says Marcia. "We've decided that life is simple. It's only our perspectives that complicate it."

In their home, as in their art, Marcia and Bill acclaim the simple perspective of free spirits. □

PASSION
IN PRACTICE

Mortar Mystery

Homeowners turn sleuths after subtle clues throw doubt on the true age of their Colonial Revival dwelling.

By Skye Alexander   Produced By Peggy Fisher

Discovery of the first subtle clue opened the door to some startling implications for Laurie Hartman and Ted Leigh. All was not as it appeared.

The couple had eagerly—perhaps a little too quickly—taken possession of their Beverly, Massachusetts, Colonial Revival home. They viewed it as a once-stately, 18th-century jewel that had fallen onto hard times. Their initial inspection was cursory, but revealed that only major renovation could restore its vigor and

Right: *Original living room woodwork includes gunstock corner posts, hand-hewn beams, and wainscoting.*
Left: *The resuscitated Colonial Revival.*
Above: *Laurie Hartman and Ted Leigh in their garden.*

Photographs: William Stites.

Mortar Mystery

Left: *The dining room's 19th-century mantel and Federal period moldings recall the style of colonial craftsman Samuel McIntire.*
Right: *The maple pencil-post bed is a reproduction, but the homespun pillows are antiques.*
Below: *Oval panels in the stairwell are original to the house.*

grace. Laurie and Ted felt qualified for the task, having already restored a Victorian house and an 1886 medicine factory.

"So, we took the plunge," Laurie says. But just as they prepared a tender attack with hammers, saws, and brushes, their carpentry was supplanted by detective work.

Evidence in the attic initially cast doubt on the house's age. Beneath floorboards, Ted found empty mortises notched in beams. There were no tenoned mates and no apparent reason for the cuts, which seemed suspicious.

"Were these beams recycled from an earlier house?" Ted wondered.

Soon, he spotted clues that siding and flooring materials were salvaged. Then came the clincher— the chimney's mortar.

Though bricks in the 12-foot-square central chimney were 300 years old, the mortar was still firm. If the chimney had been there for centuries, mortar would have crumbled with age. Was the chimney recently repointed, a process of refreshing the grout with an inch of new mortar? Or was it actually a recent chimney built with old brick?

"I had to remove three courses of brick to take a close look," says Ted. "The quality of the mortar was consistent front to back, which meant it was new construction and not a repointing

Mortar Mystery

Left: *The large kitchen dining table came from Laurie's grandmother's root cellar.*
Right: *These aren't colonial times, so kitchen appliances are up to date. Ted built the kitchen cabinets, which have raised-panel doors.*
Below: *Vegetables and herbs were grown in the garden.*

maintenance job. The house couldn't be as old as we thought. Surprising."

As the couple soon learned, the house was actually built around 1932 by antiques buffs. The original builders erected the eclectic revival edifice by combining bits and pieces gleaned from various aging buildings throughout Massachusetts and New Hampshire.

The house is a delightful mélange of architectural oddities. For instance, gunstock corner posts in the living room are curved and wider at the top than at the bottom in order to support the second story. Doors between rooms are actually two different doors mounted back to back. When closed, each one matches the rest of the details in its own room. Floorboards still bear the numbers carved into them when they were removed from their original location. (This simplified the reassembly chore.)

Rejuvenating these features proved even more arduous than determining their age. But once started, Laurie and Ted invested ample vision and labor so their house appeared to be the 18th-century reproduction it was originally intended to be.

They began by cutting down pine trees that had blocked sun from the home's moss-encased exterior for 20 years.

"When those waterlogged clapboards started to

Reviving Colonial

It's not really necessary to revive Colonial Revival architecture. It never passed away.

Perhaps because it encompasses elements of tradition, good taste, and patriotism, Colonial Revival homes have enjoyed rather steady popularity since emerging during the nation's centennial celebrations in the 1870s. Other revivals may fade,

but the faithful have never deserted this familiar, ever-evolving style.

The elements adding up to Colonial Revival are an amalgam of pieces borrowed from colonial-era housing. Most are two-story homes with formal entryways, such as columned porticos. The door is centered in the front facade and flanked by symmetrically placed double-hung windows. These features were adapted from Georgian and Federal styles, which were dominant motifs of 18th-century America.

Though many today respond warmly to the strong, certain lines of colonial-era structures, this was not always the case. Thomas Jefferson so disdained the College of William and Mary's Georgian architecture, he called it "rude misshapen piles, which, but that they have roofs, would be taken for brick kilns."

Other critics dismissed the homes of early America as "outrageous deformities to the eye of taste," "wood wens on the face of nature," and "happily . . . perishable."

However, bursting with patriotic enthusiasm during the nation's 100th anniversary, revivalists began silencing critics with a chorus of pounding hammers.

By 1916, it reached the point where architect Ralph S. Fanning wrote, "So many of our foremost architects have been working in the so-called Colonial style of architecture during the last few years and so many of the original examples of this unique style have been reproduced in publications, that this country may almost be said to be undergoing a colonial revival."

What fed this fervency? Several key factors were identified by William B. Rhoads in his book *The Colonial Revival* (Garland Publishing, Inc., 1977). These include:

● **Low cost.** The rich could build their palatial Georgian mansions. But working families also could worship at the Colonial Revival altar by building inexpensive, colonial dwellings. Wood was cheap, pattern books had standardized architectural details, and ornamentation was limited.

● **An appeal to simplicity.** The clean style was a reaction against the foppery of Victorian styles, particularly that seen in some Queen Anne extravagances.

● **A return to craftsmanship.** The style was lauded for achieving the "thoroughness of workmanship" characteristic of old New England houses. Furnituremaker Gustav Stickley praised its "honest, enthusiastic craftsmanship."

● **An escape to a carefree past.** Historian Vincent Scully noted that the revival flourished in seaside resorts of the 1870s as an escape "from an industrial civilization grown complex and brutal, from cities grown too dense and hard."

These designs also harkened back to what was romantically perceived as a more glorious past.

Rhoads writes, "The Colonial Revivalist typically saw the colonial period as a good time when people were honest, sincere, strong—in a word, virtuous." □

By Steve Cooper

Left: *Once used as a greenhouse, this conservatory is now referred to as the "sod room." Ted and Laurie installed brick and grass to give the inside room an outside feel. Beverly, Massachusetts, shop owner Doris Leonhard fashioned the begonia baskets and the home's other plant arrangements.*

dry out, they shrank and began popping off the house," Laurie says.

Before painting or staining, Laurie used bleach then ammonia to rid grimy rooms of mold. She also scooped out greasy sand between kitchen floor bricks—unearthing a few mouse skeletons.

Meanwhile, Ted pursued such projects as duplicating sections of rotted trim, building new kitchen cabinets, and repairing stone foundation weaknesses.

Just as these tenacious detectives had solved the mystery in the mortar, they also stayed the renovation course and were rewarded with success. The restored Colonial Revival inspired the couple in their business as builders of custom replicas of 18th-century houses. Once again, old and new exist side by side in harmony.

Laurie says, "Just like in our own home, we're bringing together the best of many periods.... I guess you could say we're reviving Colonial Revival." □

CAPITOLIZING ON
Collectibles

By Lisa C. Jones   Produced By Eileen A. Deymier

*Sharon Archer, wife of U.S. Rep.
Bill Archer, meshes cherished
collectibles with a hint of country
charm in their Virginia home, just
a quick drive from Capitol Hill.*

Photographs: Tim Fields

CAPITOLIZING ON
Collectibles

It began with an old bottle she found buried in the mountains of Montana. Then there was a worn drying basket, a patched quilt, an aged birdcage, and before long, literally hundreds of pieces of blue-and-white Chinese porcelain.

"They were simply all wonderful finds," recalls Sharon, a California native. "I guess collecting is just in my blood."

As a child growing up in the East Bay area near San Francisco, Sharon loved to pick up bottle scraps left at construction sites. Later, when visiting relatives in Montana, Sharon and her uncle found an old gold mining cabin tucked away in the side of a mountain.

"We wouldn't go in," Sharon says. "We'd just

stand in front of the cabin door and throw a rock; wherever the rock fell, that's where we'd start digging." The digging site yielded discards left behind by the miners.

·Once dislodged from the tight earth, the refuse of early miners became instant collectible items for Sharon—especially the old soda bottles that had small-town names embossed on them.

"You could tell they were old because of the bubbles in the glass," Sharon says.

Sharon, an art and education major in college, saw her first imported porcelain dish more than 20 years ago. She made a vow to herself that one day she would begin her own collection. And, "eventually, I did," she

says, "piece by piece." Her collection now contains several pieces of centuries-old Chinese and Japanese porcelain.

By 1983, when Sharon met Bill, a congressman from Texas, at an environmental conference in the Bay area where he was guest speaker, she had also become an avid collector of country furniture, pottery, quilts, baskets, and Eskimo carvings.

A relatively new item on her collectibles list today is the birdcage. Sharon became entranced several months ago by some imported French cages she

Above: *Treasured gems lace the Archers' entryway.*
Right: *Sharon's choice of pillows and upholstery complements her collectibles.*

CAPITOLIZING ON
Collectibles

happened to see. After perusing yard sales, she started her own collection of old wooden and wire birdcages. Now she's a proud owner of 12, some of which are 100 years old. Sharon uses the cages to adorn tabletops and walls, and she says each cage in her collection has a "particularly distinct quality."

Sharon's collections and decorating skills were called upon several months after she met Bill when they got married and bought a house in McLean, Virginia, near Capitol Hill. They needed the larger quarters for their blended family that now included seven grown children.

Originally, they were looking for an old, rambling house, but they were unable to find one in their price range. Instead, Sharon used imagination and elbow grease to make their 20-year-old house what they wanted.

The couple, who often are visited by their seven children, Texas constituents, and friends, wanted their home to convey a warm sense of hospitality for all.

"We're very informal," Sharon says. "It's important for us to have a home where family and friends feel at ease to kick off their shoes and put up their feet."

Although the size of the group may dictate what room the Archers use to entertain in their home, Sharon says that "the whole house is always open to everybody. It usually depends on where the first person plops down."

Sharon's free spirit is evidenced in her uncanny ability to find and group collectibles, match color schemes, and whip up her own decorative objects.

For example, when the Archers moved into their home, Sharon disliked the red brick fireplace in the family room, or "library," as she calls it, so she and Bill fashioned a new one from plywood with stock molding panels. They also installed French tiles around the opening. Then Sharon applied 10 coats of white paint to make sure that the coarse grain was completely covered.

Above: *Sharon refinished these unmatched French chairs.*
Right: *Frustrated by what they thought was a dull mantel, the Archers designed, installed, and painted one they liked.*

28

CAPITOLIZING ON
Collectibles

"I think we gave that fireplace personality," Sharon says.

Sanding, painting, remodeling—none of these tasks frightens Sharon. "I've always worked with my hands," she says.

But finding time between meetings, constituent visits, and other social commitments can create quite a challenge for the Archers. Yet, they often do manage to squeeze in a late hour or two for completing their household tasks.

Left: *Perched above a weathered pine storage case, this assortment of aged birdcages adds a rustic touch to the family room.*
Above: *Recurring silhouettes of blue and white create a sense of elegance throughout the Archers' home.*

"Sometimes, when we've gone out to dinner or some evening event, I can come home and paint like mad," Sharon says. "With us, it's necessary to make every minute count."

A representative for 21 years, Bill admits decorating is not his forte. But he says he doesn't mind being his wife's "assistant."

In fact, Bill routinely helps his wife with projects that would be too large for one person. (His handiness seems an appropriate reflection of his position as ranking member of the House Ways and Means Committee.)

For example, Bill custom-cut many of the shutters for the bedroom windows upstairs.

"It's wonderful to see that final visual result,"

Bill explains. "In my work, success is measured by getting legislation passed— something that isn't directly visual—but here the results are visual and different. I enjoy the collections along with her."

In addition to helping with the fireplace and the shutters, Bill installed many of the light fixtures throughout the house, plus he helped build the couple's deck.

The deck expands the house's living and entertaining space. Bill and Sharon like to eat breakfast on it, enjoying the fresh morning breeze before Bill leaves for the nation's Capitol.

"I think it's fabulous," Sharon says of the deck. "I love being outdoors."

The deck is also a nursery where Sharon

trains topiaries of myrtle and both English and American needlepoint ivy.

Bill says that there are always special moments for him to admire his wife's instinctive decorating style and her natural penchant for collecting. "She's so artistically inclined," the congressman explains, and "I'm color-blind."

Sharon feeds her passion when she accompanies Bill on international business, taking time to gather historical tidbits and collectible items.

While in China a couple of years ago, the Archers visited countryside villages where Sharon discovered women embroidering collars for their newborn grandchildren. Enraptured by the collars' handmade graces, Sharon purchased a few of her own.

"We are so fortunate to be able to travel to so many parts of the world because of Bill's job," Sharon says. "It's hard work . . . but we get a sense of so many cultures."

The Archers' living room is a panorama of world travel, bespeckled with Oriental scrolls, a host of lacquered, wooden, and stretched leather wedding boxes, temple fixtures from Thailand, French jugs, blue-and-white porcelain

Left: The three-screen painting of porcelain collectibles in the Archers' master bedroom was a gift to the couple.
Top: The cozy sitting area in the master bedroom adds an unexpected dimension.
Above right: Filtered sunlight ties together several piecemeal items in a guest room.

from China and Japan, Japanese imariware, and other items Sharon holds dear. Her oldest item is a 300-year-old wood carving from Thailand.

"Bill always says, 'You buy it, you carry it,'" Sharon says, "and I've never come home without having my arms filled to overflowing!" □

33

A HULL OF

A HOUSE

*The seas of life are calm as Jim
and Marlene Hintz find happiness in a
home patterned after a boat.*

Sometimes people can describe their desires in only the vaguest terms. They want something different. Something unusual. Something they can't quite put a finger on.

Jim and Marlene Hintz felt that way when considering the design for a new house. They hungered for a distinctive shape. But what was distinctive?

Flipping through a magazine one day, Jim experienced his architectural epiphany. There it was: a ship's-bottom house.

"Ship's bottom" perfectly describes the design's roofline, which looks like a boat hull turned upside down and plopped atop a simple Cape Cod house. Though the design offers some modest space advantages, its essential appeal is visual and visceral.

The Hintzes' shipshape home successfully captures the design's charisma. Their recently built dwelling almost seems to be sailing a cresting swell as it stands on the rise of a rolling hill in the Kettle Morraine region, about 30 miles southwest of Milwaukee, Wisconsin.

"I knew it was what I wanted the moment I saw it, even though I'd never seen a house quite like it," Jim says.

Marlene agrees. "It was so out of the ordinary," she says. "Right away, we went to the library trying to find out everything about the style."

Though information was limited, they did discover that most were built along the Massachusetts' coastline during the mid-1700s. They have always been an architectural rarity.

After their research, the couple's next step was more complicated. Building the unusual roofline required long consultation with their builder, Ed Hintz (no relation). Immediately hooked by the challenge of an unusual project, Ed followed his clients' lead and hit the books.

"How do you build a roof like that? I didn't know," says the builder. "I

⚓

Left: *With its elegantly bowed roof, this architectural style is a natural to be called ship's bottom. Cedar shingles and redwood siding enrich the house's appeal.*
Above: *Marlene and Jim Hintz sit outside their Wisconsin home.*

By Steve Cooper
Produced with Sue Mattes

had never seen one before, either, and the way we build now is not the way they built two hundred years ago along the coast."

From the beginning, the bowed rafters that would give shape to the roof were the structure's critical element. Walls and rooms below that singular roof could be conventional. But capping them required materials crafted with the strength of a Yankee clipper.

Early on, the Hintzes investigated a prefabricated kit version of a ship's-bottom house. This approach would have neatly solved the rafter problem because the factory would have supplied them. Also, for a professional builder, assembly would be relatively easy—Ed could just follow the instructions.

But the manufacturer was half a continent away. Plus, Ed felt the project would prove less complicated working with locally available materials and his list of subcontractors.

So the search began for a company capable of making curved rafter beams. Fortunately, a manufacturer in nearby Pewaukee, Wisconsin, was up to the task. It supplies laminated wood beams for architectural projects throughout the upper Midwest.

The Hintzes' roof required 44 gently arching, 22-foot beams. Each beam was constructed by gluing together eight boards and bending them into shape using huge jigs.

"They're extremely strong. In fact, the roof is twice as strong as it needs to be," says Ed, who also is a civil engineer and knows about roof stress.

Because of the steep slope, four layers of very thin cedar shingles were overlapped to enclose the roof's surface and make it watertight. Cedar is also a visually appealing complement to the home's natural redwood siding.

"It's an expensive roof, but you won't

⚓

Left: *Generous windows were designed to take advantage of the view of the lush Wisconsin countryside.*
Top: *The fireplace's back wall is slightly curved to direct heat toward the room.*
Above: *The rack for hanging pots was made for the Hintzes by a blacksmith.*

see many that look so good or perform so well," says Ed.

Below the roof, construction is the same as for most new houses. The only evidence of the ship's-bottom style can be seen in upstairs bedrooms, where walls curve with the roof.

For the home's interiors, Marlene relied on her research into mid-18th-century styles. She wanted rooms that were authentic to the design, but still comfortable for daily living.

Windows were of critical importance because they are a key architectural element to both interiors and exteriors. Marlene chose true divided windows—each individual pane in a sash is divided by wood muntins—instead of the cosmetic, snap-out grids often seen in contemporary windows.

To dress these windows, she knitted lace and selected handmade curtains and antique linens. Classically simple trim work in pine added an appropriate finishing touch.

For most floors, 8-inch pine planks were fastened down with square-headed cut nails. Though neither soft-wood floors nor bulky fasteners are favored by modern builders, they are essential to achieving the right feel in the Hintz home.

Jim says, "We know pine is soft wood, and it can be easily dented and scratched. But this floor gives us the right look,

Above: *This newel cap in the entryway was carved by a friend of the Hintzes.*

and it hasn't been as much of a problem as people think pine is."

The house has three Count Rumford-style fireplaces. This 200-year-old design has a shallow, angled firebox to thrust more heat into rooms.

Attending to all these interior details was a complex undertaking. But Marlene says, "We've tried to maintain the spirit of the times wherever possible and, with plenty of hard work, I think we succeeded."

Shopping for specialty items, such as hardware, took time.

"We searched ads in magazines like *Country Home* looking for catalogs carrying the kinds of things we needed, like light fixtures. Eventually, we were able to assemble what we wanted," Marlene says.

Through their experience, the Hintzes learned the necessity of meticulous planning. They spent as long building the plan as they spent building the house.

"The key is to find a builder who is cooperative and will go along with your ideas. We spent many afternoons going back and forth over the plans Ed drew. Always refining," Jim says.

The final result is breathtaking—a pleasing balance of form and function.

Marlene says, "It turned out exactly as I had imagined it. It's like a picture in a magazine." □

THE YARN OF THE SHIP'S-BOTTOM HOUSE

The ship's-bottom house has a nautical moniker, but the relationship between this design and oceangoing vessels is one of appearance only.

Jack Rogers, whose company, Bow House, Inc., manufactures ship's-bottom-house building kits, says, "Flamboyant writers want us to believe in this kinship between these houses and the sea. But it's not so. It's purely romantic hype."

True, the 10 remaining examples built between the late 1600s and early 1800s were all constructed within easy reach of the sea around Cape Cod. Then, there's the shape; it's so strikingly similar to a ship's hull turned upside down that it's been assumed the builders were shipwrights. But that idea doesn't hold water.

The two best-known examples were actually built by the farmers who occupied them. They

simply adapted standard roof-raising techniques to create the distinctive arch.

The earliest roof still remaining crowns the Seconesset Homestead, built in 1678 in Falmouth, Massachusetts. But no one knows why the ship's-bottom style was chosen.

It is evident that colonial homeowners enjoyed variety in rooflines. A 1932 essay on early American roofs identified 15 separate roof shapes fitted to the Cape Cod design. In addition to the ship's-bottom, roof styles included rounded rainbows, complex double-hipped, and saltbox.

Of them all, the ship's-bottom stirs strongest emotions, says Lynne O'Connor, of Russell Swinton Oatman Design Associates, Inc., which offers plans for building the shipshape house.

She says, "It's the kind of style that people seem to either love or hate." □

Above: *The skeleton of the Hintzes' roofline is a series of graceful, laminated pine rafters.*

April

Leading to the heart of the home (the kitchen), a side porch celebrates life and country with ferns, flowers, a flag, and rustic twig furniture.

Youngs
AT HEART

Once just a showcase for his furniture company, Jeff Young's North Carolina farmhouse now has a focus on family, too.

For Jeff Young, moving into the farmhouse of his dreams on 150 acres of prime North Carolina rolling grasslands wasn't the happy day one would have expected from the storybook setting. His first marriage had just ended in divorce, and his heart was too empty to muster much enthusiasm for decorating the spacious 12-year-old home only for himself and visits from his young daughter and teenage son, who would now be living with their mother.

The designers he hired to do the job for him produced picture-perfect interiors, but, somehow, something was missing. *Jeff* was missing. The home was a beautiful shell without a heart.

But things changed. Visiting the home today, one gets no sense of vacuous spaces that are merely inhabited by rote, not lived in at all.

The farmhouse pulsates with life—and love. The stadium-size kitchen (only a minor exaggeration—this kitchen is the kind many a chef would die for) no longer is deafeningly still, its state-of-the-art

BY CANDACE ORD MANROE

40

Photographs: William N. Hopkins, Hopkins Associates.
Furniture throughout is from Lexington Furniture Industries.

Left: The blended family of Lynn and Jeff Young includes twins Jeffrey (far left) and Christopher Shaw, and Annie Young. Not shown is Jeff's son, Patrick, away on a school trip.

41

Top: *The Youngs' kitchen marries sleek, high-tech appliances with down-to-earth activity in a pleasing way. Children's art adorns the refrigerator, and breakfast makings await attention on the island.*
Above: *Most family meals are eaten at this kitchen table.*

appliances begging to hum and heat.

Instead, Jeff's new wife, Lynn, is busy washing and chopping vegetables for another of the home-cooked meals she prepares for Jeff and her twin boys, Jeffrey and Christopher Shaw, and on weekends, Jeff's daughter, Annie, and his son, Patrick.

When Jeff gets home from his job heading up Lexington Furniture Industries (he's chief operating officer), it's not emptiness he finds waiting, but the smell of fresh vegetables sautéeing in the kitchen. The listlessness of his not-so-distant bachelor days has been transformed into liveliness—how could it be otherwise, with two eager 6-year-olds awaiting the sound of his car, anxious to drag him off to the barn to see the horses?

"Life is much different from when I first moved here," Jeff understates. "Much better."

These days, the home is alive with activity, the majority of which is centered in the kitchen. In the breakfast nook, from the comfortable vantage point of casual Windsor chairs with a warm rag rug underfoot, the family has their meals—sometimes with up to 12 different species of birds feeding in the birdhouse just outside the large bay window.

"We can watch them, and it's as if there is no separation between indoors and outdoors," says Lynn.

At any time between meals, the favorite indoor retreat is the kitchen sitting area. With the

Just behind the breakfast nook, a cozy sitting area appeals with its pure country style—a collection of pewter in the corner cupboard and a print of a Bob Timberlake painting above the mantel. After meals, the family enjoys gathering around the hearth in winter or enjoying a fresh breeze in summer.

Far from the hands-off showhouse it originally appeared to be when Jeff Young, as a bachelor, first moved in, the home now overflows with life. The basement family room blends American Indian-influenced upholstery, a display-case coffee table, and a miniature store with the real stuff of life—a large TV and a load of toys.

Even the more formal living room smacks of family life now, with photos adding a personal handprint to a new library table.

hearth as the focal point, the room beckons with its homey dove-and-heart woven fabrics on soft seating, scattered with pillows and throws.

"But one of the benefits of living on a farm," says Jeff, "is that you spend the vast majority of your time outdoors."

Often, this means enjoying the day from a comfortable perch on the old-fashioned wraparound porch, where wicker and twig rocking chairs invoke the best of Southern hospitality.

The new life Jeff and Lynn have made together is a Cinderella story, but one that Lynn, at least, didn't believe would ever reach a happy ending.

"Jeff Young [Lynn always refers to her husband by his full name—initially, to distinguish him from her son, Jeff, later as something of a joke, and now purely out of habit] and I had a blind date in April 1990—my first date after 14 years of marriage," says Lynn. "I thought it was the perfect date, except for one thing. Five months went by, and I hadn't heard from him."

But one day she received a letter of apology—and good explanation—from Jeff. They had their second date in September. In December, they were engaged, then married in March.

"It was fast, and it was right," says Lynn.

Her instincts had not been wrong. Both professionals, both

The master bedroom, with its reproduction poster bed and Windsor chair, bespeaks old-fashioned Southern charm.

committed to family as the foundation of life, both with a fine balance of hospitality and reserve, Jeff and Lynn had too much in common not to notice one another. But not entirely a mutual admiration society, they do entertain at least one friendly rivalry: She's a graduate of Duke; he's an alum of competitor Wake Forest.

Having left her career in human resources to devote her time to mothering and managing a household, Lynn assists Jeff when they entertain his company's business associates and clients.

And now, he not only has the house, but the heart to entertain well.

The entire home is outfitted in pieces from one of his furniture company's collections—a country line by North Carolina artist Bob Timberlake that's based on favorite antiques and handcrafts Bob grew up with. These refrains of rural Carolina heritage are especially appropriate for a Carolina farmhouse. The rugged pieces practically dare the twins to do damage, while at the same time, they're unabashedly good for business.

When Jeff lived alone, the home looked something like a furniture showroom—impeccable, but not too realistic. Now his, her, and their photos spill over a library table in the living room. At last, the basement family room fits its name, strewn with toys, a trike, a big TV.

Finally, the farmhouse has a family to go along with its furniture. Finally, it's a home with a heart. □

An upstairs guest bedroom is rendered romantic with its white-on-white walls, shutters, linens, carpet, and upholstery fabrics. The space also appears deceptively vintage, thanks to a turned bed, needlepoint rug, carved mirror, and graceful highboy—all reproductions.

IN THE
Warmth
OF THE
Sun

**Summer seems endless at Michael and Karen Zacha's horse
ranch in the hills above Malibu, California.**

Left: *The eclectic blend
in Michael and Karen
Zacha's living room
mixes a saddlebag from
the Middle East draped
across a chair, Mexican
masks, Egyptian sofa
pillows, and an
armoire.*

Imagine a horse ranch overlooking a
prime stretch of the Golden State's
coastline, and it might look something like
the home of Michael and Karen Zacha.

Seemingly all glass, warm tiles, and sunny
colors, the ranch has the attitude of a
thoroughbred. The dwelling fulfills every
task with grace and ease.

It wasn't always so on the Zacha spread.
When Michael purchased the property in
1971, there was no two-story structure with
three barns, a pool, and 200 acres of lemon
trees, avocado trees, and rolling-hill
pasturelands for horses.

"When I first saw it, the house as it stood

BY BARBARA JEAN NEAL AND STEVE COOPER

Above: *Karen and
Michael are as fond of
horses as their children,
Andrew, 13, Caitlin, 5,
and Chase, 3, are. Their
ranch already houses 31
horses, and they are
expanding again to
include a new barn and
a horse-training arena.*

Left: *Michael jettisoned
aluminum windows
along this dining room
wall to make way for
three pairs of glazed
French doors.*

Interior and patio photographs: Ken Bell. Above photographs of family
and exterior: Dale Berman.

49

Above: *Since his days as a used-furniture trader in the 1960s, Michael has kept special finds for himself, such as this century-old crazy quilt in the home's entry.*

IN THE
Warmth
OF THE
Sun

was this totally out-of-place little tract house, and it looked like somebody helicoptered it in. . . . The whole area around the house was red-painted asphalt. It was a mess," says Michael, a professional builder.

So Michael set to work ripping up asphalt, expanding rooms, erecting an upper story, and punching holes into walls wherever a window or French doors would fit.

"It's grown and expanded and changed as my needs have changed," says Michael. "I bought it when I was single, and now we're married and have three children. So it has evolved through different kinds of needs."

For example, when the upper story was added, it had a bedroom, a bathroom, and another huge, open room. Three years ago, the open room was partitioned to create another bedroom and bath. Now the top floor has three bedrooms, a studio, and will soon include another large bath.

"Nothing is ever really finished around here," Michael says.

While he attended to structural changes, Karen turned her artistic eye to decor.

"We have a very outdoorsy life-style that's centered around our kids and horses and dogs and other animals," says Karen, who works as an illustrator when she isn't busy with equestrian dressage events. "We tend to be the kind of people who come into the house with mud on our riding boots. So this has to be an informal, relaxed place."

Right: *While shopping in Guadalajara, Mexico, Karen spotted the rich material now covering the dining table. The tablecloth is a subtle connection to the coast's Hispanic heritage.*

Above: *Entertaining is a party in this open kitchen. "The dining room and kitchen were separate," says Karen. "So, we opened them up to make it all one space. Friends feel at home."*

Left: *Though the Pacific Ocean lies only two miles downhill from the back patio, the Zacha hilltop home was built at an elevation of 1,700 feet.*

Above: *An authentic, wood-and-leather stagecoach trunk sits at the foot of the Zachas' bed. Michael says, "The junk dealer I got it from was asking twenty-five dollars, but I got him to come down to five. It's one of my prized possessions."*

For easy care, there are Mexican paver tiles for the entrance, living room, dining room, and kitchen. Area rugs add color.

In the living room, Karen sometimes uses slipcovers for sofa and chairs. This allows frequent restyling without the major expense of purchasing new furniture.

Throughout the house, she has placed carved horses from Michael's collection from Guadalajara, Mexico, to add a light touch. They stand as a whimsical counterpoint to such distinctive furnishings as a 100-year-old English confectioner's table in the entry, a turn-of-the-century dining room cabinet, and an elegant living room corner armoire.

"Karen is a very creative, artistic person. She is constantly changing things around, and that's what I like about her—her sense of fun and the way she allows her childlike quality to work through her sense of design," Michael says.

For Karen, designing for a country life means creating a home similar to the farm in Toronto, Canada, where she spent summers while growing up.

"Our children are fortunate to be living in the best of both worlds here. We're only forty-five minutes from a huge city, Los Angeles, and all it offers. Yet, here at home we have our ponies and chickens and rabbits. They can even see rattlesnakes and coyotes. It's absolutely country," she says. □

Above: *The Zachas' nightstand is a stack of metal-lined Oriental boxes. Perched around them are some of Karen's animal statues.*

IN THE
Warmth
OF THE
Sun

53

Refeathering the
N·E·S·T

After their grown children moved out, a Minnesota couple refashioned their home in a style that soars.

Coping with an empty nest is one of the chief occupational hazards of parenting.

For two decades and

longer, parents' lives are largely shaped by the needs and activities of their children. For many, limited resources force interior design considerations into the background as family funds are siphoned off for back-to-school wardrobes, orthodontist's bills, weekly grocery trips, and an endless array of toys and other diversions.

So, when the three children of Leon and Cynthia Moat moved out of the family's Owatonna, Minnesota, home to establish their own lives, the couple had to decide: What do we do now?

The answer became a turning point for Cynthia, who radically altered the personality of her contemporary ranch home and turned it into a haven of early Americana.

"This came just at the right time for me," says Cynthia, who launched into the extensive remodeling project in 1987. "With the children grown and gone, I needed to do something for myself. It's been an accomplishment. I think it says, 'Yes, you can do it for yourself.'"

In the beginning, Leon had serious misgivings about the extensive transformation of the

BY STEVE COOPER
PRODUCED BY PAT CARPENTER

Right: *Most of the carefully selected furnishings in this keeping room are from the 19th century, including the blue painted cupboard from New York, the 1860 rocker with its original paint, the Hepplewhite candlestand, and the shoe-foot settle. The mantel is an oak beam salvaged from an old building.*

Top left: *The limestone pathway was made with locally quarried material.*

Bottom left: *Leon and Cynthia Moat await customers in their home's modest antiques shop.*

•••

Photographs: William N. Hopkins, Hopkins Associates

Refeathering the
N·E·S·T

home where the family has lived for more than 25 years. He feared the strong style statement might hurt resale value, should they ever decide to move.

"It didn't make a lot of sense to me until people—friends and neighbors—started coming over after we were well along in the process," says Leon, a

retired schoolteacher. "So many of them would come through and they'd 'ooh' and 'ah' and really get caught up in it all. That's when I began to understand and appreciate what Cynthia was doing."

The remodeling began when Cynthia spotted a painted pie safe in a shop. The shape and color appealed to her instantly. But when she took the pie safe home, she discovered the cupboard's blue paint didn't mesh with her kitchen's decor.

"At that time, my house was all oak and frills, and pictures on the wall, and carpeting," says Cynthia. "No matter how I arranged the room, the pie safe just didn't quite fit. But I was hooked. Those rooms were going to change because that pie safe was staying put."

Right: Leon nailed the redwood ceiling in place. The salvaged lumber came from an old hotel. "It gives rooms a color and character you just couldn't get from new wood," he says. The authenticity of age also sets apart the room's antiques, including the comb-back Windsor rocker from the early 1800s and the 1830 dining table.

Top left: A collection of hand-carved duck decoys hangs from the keeping-room mantel.

Bottom left: Cynthia and Leon put wainscoting on dining room walls to give them distinction. Other rooms have a chair rail only.

•••

Refeathering the
N·E·S·T

Left: *When Cynthia
began repainting
the kitchen cabinets
back in 1987, she
knew she was
making a
commitment to a
major remodeling
project. "There was
no going back after
that," she says.
Another big step
was having wood
installed over
laminated plastic
counters. The
kitchen's 18th-
century sawbuck
table has a blue
base with a
scrubbed top and
rosehead nails.*

Right: *This pie safe,
still coated in its
original blue, was
the first of the
painted pieces
Cynthia bought for
the house.*

● ● ●

Soon, she was selling
more contemporary oak
pieces, both to make way
for older, painted furniture
and to help underwrite the
transition. Other changes
involved painting kitchen
cabinets and adding pine
flooring, wainscoting, and
redwood ceilings.

Though he was not a
carpenter, Leon waded into
a variety of remodeling
projects, including
renovating a recently built
family room addition and
installing pine planks over
oak floors in the bedroom.

"I wasn't always sure we
were doing the right thing
by tearing everything up
and doing things like
covering oak with pine.
But as time has gone by, I
think I've become as
addicted to the changes as
Cynthia is," Leon says.

The authentic American
look wasn't achieved
overnight. For Cynthia, it
has been as evolutionary
as it has been
revolutionary.

"I love decorating, but I
knew nothing about
arranging these pieces. So
we brought them in, and I
would rearrange them over
and over and over again,"
she says.

Leon recalls mornings
when he would discover
Cynthia had awakened in
the night and spent hours
rearranging things. Fresh
scratches in the floor were
clues to her late-night
activities.

She says, "Most of the
time, it was a laughing
matter, but now it all fits
together beautifully."

Along the way, the
Moats shuffled rooms, too.

Refeathering the
N·E·S·T

Left: *Bedrooms remain true to the Moats' Early American vision. The spool rope bed is dated 1848. Hanging over the mortised-and-pegged blanket rack at the foot of the bed is a homespun blanket made in Massachusetts about 1850. Leon made the window shutters in both bedrooms from tongue-and-groove bead board. They offer privacy and, on cold nights, insulation against a winter chill. Cynthia found stenciling wall accents one of the easiest aspects of the project.*

Right: *Horizontal planking gives these bedroom walls a sense of age.*

• • •

The family room addition became a keeping room, and the home's living room was made over into a spacious dining room.

The rooms were furnished with 18th- and 19th-century finds, including rope beds, a spinning wheel, painted cupboards, and folk art.

"I'm not quite certain why I wanted this style so much," says Cynthia. "It just makes me feel comfortable. But it takes a certain amount of courage to do something like this when you live in a fairly typical, middle-class neighborhood. You're being different, and that's always somewhat risky at first."

But neighbors were soon won over. Now Leon helps friends who want pine floors for their own homes. And, putting her ever-expanding knowledge to work, Cynthia opened a home-based antiques shop.

"The great thing about having the shop is that the education has been tremendous. It requires quite a bit of research, and that's been very enjoyable. And my timing couldn't have been better. I don't have time now to feel the void of the empty nest," she says.

Remodeling has had another unexpected benefit: It's drawn the couple closer together.

"Doing a project like this helps you find out more about each other," says Leon. "Like the way Cynthia tackled plastering walls, which is something I didn't want any part of. She did a fantastic job on that. Through this whole project she's shown a lot of determination."

Such fresh insights have helped the couple realize something about the empty nest. It doesn't have to be so empty after all. □

61

Nuances of NORMANDY

*Monique Shay, a native of
Normandy, France,
recaptures the grace of early
French crafts in the colorful,
earthy antiques and
accessories she displays in her
home and antiques shop.*

Photographs: Jon Jensen.

Left: *Monique renovated this 19th-century farmhouse.*

Right: *Cascading beds of herbs, annuals, and perennials encompass this garbage shed.*

Nuances of NORMANDY

A long time has passed since Monique Shay lived near the gentle hills and quiet streams of her native Normandy, France, where the sight of frugal farmers carving supper tables, cupboards, and other wooden wares seemed commonplace.

Today, more than 30 years later, Monique retains bits and pieces of the French countryside in her home and antiques store in Woodbury, Connecticut.

Settling first in the heart of New Canaan, Monique eventually moved to Stamford where she married and raised five boys and two girls.

She was living in Stamford when she bought her first antique, an armoire she saw in a Canadian farmer's barn. Monique liked the armoire's detailed raised and diamond-pointed panels, tailored cornices, and mitered corners— many of the traits of early French pieces.

Her interest having been piqued, Monique began traveling (when the tasks of child rearing permitted) across the Canadian border—more than 400 miles north of Connecticut—in hopes of finding other vestiges of a time long gone.

In the early 17th century, French citizens—looking for greater political freedoms—had made their way to Canada via the St. Lawrence River. Many of them had fled with only a few possessions.

The farmers among them had brought both farming and crafts skills. They

BY LISA C. JONES
PRODUCED BY BONNIE MAHARAM

discovered that the fruitwoods used by their forefathers in France were a scarcity in the new land. So, they turned to pinewood to craft their wares.

The settlers also adopted the Canadians' custom of painting furniture with untempered shades of primarily red, yellow, green, and blue. The Canadians, who painted their furniture and their houses in bright tones, used the boisterous colors to cheer up the harsh winters, as well as to add a delightful finish to the pine grain. Eventually, the French-styled cornices and panels were integrated with the Canadians' use of color to form a unique French Canadian folk art.

Over the years, Monique's journeys to Canada yielded many rustic furnishings similar in spirit to the carved items she recalled so vividly as a child.

"I grew up with antiques," Monique says with a heavy French accent. "I've always liked old things."

Monique had her choice of some of the best pieces when she began buying—and at reasonable prices. "At that time," Monique explains, "nobody wanted those things, and they cost only a few dollars."

As a matter of fact, many of the Canadian farmers laughed at Monique for hauling away the old furniture they stashed in their barns as rubble. But with time, that sentiment changed. "In the past few years, the Canadians have begun to

Nuances of NORMANDY

Above: *Monique combs Canadian regions for antique items, such as this 19th-century high chair and checkerboard.* Left: *Most of Monique's colorful pieces of pottery come from the Alps region of France.* Right: *Mellow tones, rustic furnishings, and decorative decoys fill the living room with warmth.*

Left: *These rare pieces of jaspé pottery from Monique's personal collection are known for their exquisite multi-color finish.* Right: *A sizable farm table anchors the dining room, which is furnished with a selection of ornate antiques similar to those found in Monique's shop.*

collect their own antiques," Monique says, "so they have become much more rare and expensive." In her shop, Monique says pottery may start at $50 and early cupboards may go for $15,000.

Yet, price doesn't keep ardent collectors away. Renowned fashion designers, entertainers, and serious antiques collectors are among Monique's regular clientele. And having made a reputable name for her merchandise simply by word of mouth, many of Monique's furnishings can be spotted throughout the United States, Europe, and Israel.

When Monique moved to Woodbury in 1981, she was greeted by a dilapidated Greek Revival farmhouse and barn. Both of the 1814 structures were in shambles.

But a collapsing roof, crumbling plastered walls, faulty wiring, and untamed landscaping failed to dampen Monique's spirits. "I love to take something old and bring life to it," she says. Besides, Monique felt an inexplicable connectedness between the environs of her Woodbury home and the serenity of her native land.

"I knew what I wanted," she says. "The historical district of Woodbury reminds me of the French countryside in Normandy where I grew up."

Using the barn behind her house as a showroom, Monique, who works with her oldest daughter (also named Monique but who prefers to be called Monique, Jr.), set up Monique Shay Antiques and Design.

Monique, Jr. says she remembers the many times she and her siblings accompanied Monique to Canada while she scavenged for antique goods. Like her mother, Monique, Jr. took an early interest in primitive French art forms.

"I love the feel of the furniture," she says. "It's impressionistic, and I like the cheery colors."

The natural farm setting of Monique's antiques shop—part of a working poultry farm in the 1960s—serves as a fitting backdrop for her collection of predominantly 19th-century antiques. Inside, stout farm tables, primitive setback cupboards, and aged armoires grace the floor. The shop also boasts an engaging array of handmade rawhide chairs, sideboards, butter churns, French pottery, and wooden checkerboards.

Monique buys most of her antiques from Quebec, Nova Scotia, and New Brunswick. In each area, farms, barns, convents, and old basements are thoroughly explored in order to find authentic French Canadian antique furnishings. Quarterly trips to the southeastern regions of France provide Monique with a stunning selection of marbled and flower-printed pottery.

Nuances of
NORMANDY

The carefully carved furnishings and French pottery wares in Monique's collection reflect the simple elegance of the farmers and artisans who created them centuries ago. And, Monique adds, "No two pieces are ever the same."

Monique says she never thought her antiques business, which began as a hobby, would become such an integral part of her life. "It's much more than a business," she says, after selling antiques for more than 10 years. "This place really feels like home to me now."

A sense of 19th-century charm mingles comfortably with the best of modern-day beauty in the corridors of Monique's restored home.

Monique, Jr. says her mother has an enduring sense of style. "She tries to make things look like they've been there forever," the daughter notes.

Pallor-toned walls, earthenware pottery, and the worn, muted shades of French Canadian furniture endow the huge farmhouse with a timeless, warm, and inviting glow.

A blend of French and French Canadian cultures beautifully unfolds in Monique's home. Handmade original and reproduction Canadian rugs generously cover the floors; 18th-century setback cupboards line the front foyer; and pieces of painted French pottery dot the windows of antique pantries and cupboards.

Left: *Stocked with French and Canadian implements, the kitchen is a mosaic of form and function.*
Above: *Centuries later, original hues still brighten this rattail-hinged armoire.*
Right: *Monique's walls and trim bear the primary shades used by American colonists and early French Canadians in the 17th century.*

Monique's remodeled kitchen maintains a French Canadian air with its festoons of French pottery and other dated trinkets looming above the range and a host of French copper cookware decorating a far wall. Nestled in the corner sits one of her favorite antiques.

"It's very unusual and Canadian," Monique says of the emerald green bin once used to store dry goods. "It's early, nice, and still has its original color." She guesses that the bin, with French labels such as *"ris"* (rice), *"sucre,"* (sugar), and *"café"* (coffee) was made in 1875.

"I could have sold that piece a thousand times, but it is one of my favorite possessions," she says.

When Monique isn't serving the public fine antiques, she's probably cooking a succulent dish for her family.

"I love to cook for myself and for my family," she says, "especially in the summer when all of the vegetables are ripe in the herb and flower garden." Savory herbs, annuals, and perennials make up Monique's private bouquet.

Monique, Jr. says her mother especially enjoys preparing paella—a saffron-flavored dish stuffed with rice, meat, seafood, and vegetables and herbs from the garden—for their family.

But whether it's whipping up a traditional family favorite or wooing customers with choice French and French Canadian antiques, Monique's enchantment with familial and cultural ties inevitably shines through. ☐

Nuances of NORMANDY

Above: *Dipped in saucy Canadian colors years ago, these antique butter churns offer a sweet alternative to the nightstand.*
Right: *Set in front of Monique's barn, this wooden water silo serves as a pool house.*

June

PAST TIMES

Small in size but rich with history, a Minnesota stone house radiates warmth on the weekends.

A soft summer breeze lifts the feather-light arms of the willow tree toward the open sky. The branches fall, gently brushing against the aged stone cottage owned by St. Paul-area real estate agent Sam Fudenberg and enjoyed for family retreats.

A car slowly makes its way up the gravel entrance, interrupting the stillness of the tiny, unincorporated town of Wasioja, Minnesota, a township too small to have a grocery store, post office, or gas station to call its own.

It is the week's end, and Sam fires up the charcoal grill, chills a few glasses for iced tea, and awaits the arrival of his children, Brenda and Brian, who are meeting him at the cottage for some relaxation.

Together they will gear down from the hectic week by hiking along nearby wooded trails, bicycling on the winding country roads, or playing a host of games, such as lawn darts, croquet, and Sam's favorite, archery, on the lawn.

"Time changes once you turn down that road," says Sam's son, Brian. "The activity level here is low." An accounts manager

Top: *Sam (center) and children Brenda and Brian steal a moment of rest from a game of croquet.*
Above: *Leather-bound scrapbooks chronicle the changing face of this 19th-century cottage.*
Right: *In harmony with its past and the present, this 1858 Greek Revival home is an ideal retreat for Sam and his family.*

BY LISA C. JONES
PRODUCED WITH JEAN LEMMON

at the same company as his father, Brian enjoys simply relaxing on the front porch warmed by the sun.

Brenda, a marketing director who lives in Minneapolis, also appreciates the tranquil setting of the small town. "You entertain yourself," she says. "When I'm here, I like to take walks and read romantic novels." For Brenda, the cottage offers "a great getaway from the hustle and bustle of the city."

But for their father, the 19th-century Greek Revival home—used as an antiques store by the previous owners—offers much more than an occasional weekend escape.

What began as an inspiration for a weekend retreat in 1986—when Sam got his first glimpse of the small stone cottage on his way to a neighboring town—instantly became a passion.

A meticulous collector and hobbyist, Sam was "awestruck" by the 1858 structure, and says that he knew that its small confines would bring together "the different feels" of his interests and collections.

A professional archer in the early '70s, Sam has since delved into everything from making buckskins to collecting antique guns and turn-of-the-century office furniture.

Left: A decoy finds a home nesting atop an 1840s drop-leaf table in the dining room.
Above: The excavation of the front porch yielded this stunning array of weathered apothecary bottles.
Below: Sam's fascination with the early American frontier is seen in such pieces as the pine pedestal and turn-of-the-century hotel register swivel stand equipped with an antique register and pen.

PAST TIMES

Top: *Fine oak and marble set the turn-of-the-century-styled bathroom aglow.*
Bottom: *At Sam's request, carpenters hand-scribed wooden trim to fit the rugged edges of the exposed wall in the kitchen. The beautiful stone walls were hidden under a layer of plaster.*

Before long, the restful little retreat, became Sam's obsession.

"I go wild," Sam unabashedly explains of his fascination with the historic stone cottage listed on the National Historical Register in 1975.

"I bought this house as a getaway—with no intention to restore it," Sam says. But after searching through reams of historical accounts of Andrew Doig, the Scottish immigrant who built the modest house 134 years ago, Sam launched into what became a five-year restoration project.

A stickler for details, Sam contracted local carpenters to ensure that the furnishings and the structure accurately reflected the 19th-century frontier. Now, the restored cottage boasts its original pine floors and pegged doors. Antique kerosene lamps—some of which were once used in train cabins—have been wired for electricity. And, frontier survey maps grace the lath and plaster walls.

The restoration gave way to another project for Sam—making a record of its past. "I'm a memorabilia type of person," he says, showing off three leather-bound albums of memoirs of the original cottage and townspeople, plus news clippings.

Purchasing the cottage off County Road 16 has enhanced Sam's life, and he says he hopes the little stone cottage "will be around at least another forty years for others to enjoy long after I'm gone." □

The beauty of the 19th-century frontier streams through the dining area. An 1874 butternut table and matching splint chair set, a wood box brimming with logs for a fire, and spare window treatments that let in the light are just a few reasons Sam's cottage has the makings of a relaxing weekend.

SUN STROKES

Illustrator Mary Engelbreit and family perfect the fine art of relaxation in their sun-brushed cottage.

Centuries before the first westbound pioneers stopped to refresh their horses and splash their own dusty faces in the bubbling stream, Beaver Spring served as watering grounds for Native Americans. Rivers and streams played an integral part in American Indian ritual, and a cool immersion into Beaver Spring no doubt was a source of spiritual, as well as physical, renewal.

It remains so even today.

Though civilization has assigned Beaver Spring and its rural surrounds to the Steelville, Missouri, postal area, it thankfully hasn't tampered with the site's original function. Artist Mary Engelbreit and her husband, Philip Delano, now own the 387 wooded acres through which the spring-fed stream laces, and they say the old watering grounds indeed nourish the soul.

With their sons, Evan, 11, and Will, 9, Mary and Phil use the property for the three R's of renewal, reflection, relaxation—goals the first

BY CANDACE ORD MANROE
PRODUCED BY MARY ANNE THOMSON

Top: *Illustrator Mary Engelbreit teams up with husband Philip Delano and sons Will (on left) and Evan for a different kind of creativity, come summer.*
Left: *Resting on 387 acres that include an old American Indian watering hole just yards away, the home permits outdoor living thanks to a new porch.*
Above: *Mary treats her collectibles to an artful composition.*

Photographs: William N. Hopkins, Hopkins Associates

A passion for blue and white, which the family doesn't indulge in their permanent residence, is given free expression in their vacation home's living room—an upbeat mix of polka dots, stripes, and checks. The coffee-table bench may be the couple's oldest purchase together: They bought it while dating 15 years ago.

Americans could relate to in spirit, if not in language.

"This used to be the big springs for area Indians," says Mary, "and the boys explore the trails, collecting arrowheads. They love to play in the pond and the creek, and we all enjoy fishing when we have the time." With a stone path leading from the house to the stream, only yards away, the rejuvenating presence of water is not just an occasional treat, but a constant source of pleasure. "Just being around the water is relaxing," says Mary.

The family heads to the vacation property from their year-round residence in Webster Groves (outside of St. Louis), 80 miles away, whenever time permits—"which isn't often enough," admits Mary. Still, "it's a great place to have parties and entertain in the country."

It also is a retreat from daily routine. For Mary, this means escaping from painting the whimsical greeting cards that have made her famous. "I paint while I'm there, but furniture, not illustrations," she says, laughing. A vacation house, after all, is intended for fun in the sun, not a lot of indoor activity—and certainly not for work.

Phil discovered the property during a canoe trip on the Meramec River. "The For Sale sign I saw

SUN STROKES

Above: *Mary reworked the living room's plain white Victorian vanity with paint, then covered its small glass panels with Victorian prints.*
Below: *Using the reverse side of fabric gives the bedroom's old easy chair an antique look.*

actually was for another, more spectacular house, which proved to be too expensive," he says. "But the agent told me about this house on the other side of the street, which included a lot more land but needed a little work."

The real estate agent's warning was an understatement. The house needed more than a little work. Built in the 1930s, it had been abandoned for years and was nothing short of a mess. But to an optimistic eye, it had potential. Plus, it came with a hundred-year-old cabin not far from its door, which immediately won Mary's heart (and which, since purchasing the property, she has used as a charming place for storing her garden equipment).

For the house itself, a new roof, bathroom, and heating and air conditioning had to be added just to make it livable.

Knowing they would want to enjoy the stream as much as possible, the couple also made one of their immediate priorities the building of a porch across the full span of house as a comfortable vantage point.

With structural matters resolved, it wasn't long before Mary used her artist's eye to transform the cottage into a real-life scene as cheerful as one of her greeting cards.

"The kitchen had horrible peeling linoleum—it was really bad—but I

SUN STROKES

· ·

Left: *Charming cabinets compensated for the kitchen's down-at-the-heels linoleum. A new backsplash and old stove set the country tone.*
Above: *A hanging pine cabinet adds character to the kitchen, along with a clock Mary outfitted with checks.*
Below: *The large porch added by Mary and Phil overlooks Beaver Spring.*

SUN
STROKES

. . . .

Above: *Mary cheered up the bathroom
by painting its medicine cabinet blue
with a small flower design and bringing
in favorite trinkets—wooden flowers
and a birdhouse.*
Below: *Bright striped comforters
in the boys' room pick up colors from the
rocking chair Mary painted.*

liked the cute cabinets," recalls
Mary. The addition of tiles, an old
Magic Chef stove, and collections of
birdhouses, cards, prints, small toys,
and tins transforms the space
completely.

Mary's sense of color is clear at
once. And she hasn't been shy about
dipping into the paints to change any
furnishing into something more
creative and fun.

The living room is a lively tale of
blue-and-white polka dots, stripes,
and checks.

"I don't have any blue in my house
in Webster, so I decided to do the
country house in blues and pale
colors," she says.

Even the medicine cabinet in the
bathroom and the back porch itself
bear Mary's colorful handiwork.

To the multifarious spaces she
adds collections—any and everything
that appeals to her. "It's a disease—
it's sick—but collecting is what I do
for relaxation or when I need
inspiration," Mary says.

"I like everything," she explains.
"I appreciate different styles,
different colors, and I throw it all
together and hope for the best."

It's wishful thinking that's paid
off. The vacation house, like Beaver
Spring that laps just outside its door,
is a magical place to rest the body
and revive the soul. □

*Cottage romance flavors the master bedroom with its brass and iron bed covered
with a '40s bedspread and piled high with chintz and crocheted pillows, then crowned with a collection of hats on the wall.
A quilt top covers the bedside table. Mary painted the adjacent stool with cherries for a touch of whimsy.*

PEDAL PUSHERS

After discovering Nantucket Island's bike paths, a Boston couple geared up to build this cozy cottage.

S itting on the deck of their Nantucket Island cottage, Bob Vogel and Barbara Pfister bask in their good fortune as waves of salty sea air wash over them.

Since first visiting Nantucket in 1984, they have been smitten with the island. The prosperous home port of America's whaling industry in the 1840s, it is now an outpost of New England quaintness 30 miles out to sea off Cape Cod.

"Nantucket is such an extraordinary place," says Bob. "From the first time we came here to ride around on bikes, I have been impressed by the island, its beaches, and moors. It's not the kind of place where you have to rush around doing things. We come to relax."

Now, after six years of planning and labor, they have constructed a personal retreat for weekends and vacations. Their primary residence remains in Brookline, Massachusetts, near Bob's work as a computer systems auditor and Barbara's duties as a business manager.

BY STEVE COOPER
PRODUCED WITH SUE MATTES

Left: *The sparse surroundings of the cottage recall a description of Nantucket Island found in Herman Melville's* Moby Dick: *"Nantucket! Take out your map and look at it... a mere hillock, and elbow of sand; all beach, without a background."*
Top: *Bob Vogel and Barbara Pfister favor bicycles for island transportation.*
Above: *A model ship Bob built recalls the island's once-mighty whaling fleet.*

Photographs: Judith Watts. Additional interior design: Joseph Boehm. Builder: Cottage Industries.
Deck furniture: Pier 1 Imports.

PEDAL PUSHERS

"But, of course," Bob says, "we're out here on the island every weekend in summer, during vacations, and over the holidays. Every chance we can get."

Their 650-square-foot, Cape Cod-style cottage has a beauty rooted in rugged simplicity, much like the island on which it nests. The shingle-sided home offers the couple a friendly haven in much the same way as the island's protective Great Harbor has embraced sailors from the time of the whalers to this day of the pleasure craft.

Off-islanders, like Bob and Barbara, are drawn by Nantucket's stark beauty. Approaching the island by sea, visitors are struck by how low in the water the 13-mile-wide oasis seems to sit. Scraped clean when long-ago glaciers receded, the landscape is as flat as a Midwestern farm field. For bicyclists, it's a smooth and easy ride to any of the windswept, sandy beaches.

Equally appealing is the harbor town and its captivating collection of more than 800 structures predating the Civil War. The town beckons strollers with its multitude of shops, museums, and history.

Barbara says, "I fell in love with the island from the first moment I

Above: *A weekend house needs easy-care seating like these painted Windsor chairs. The model bike is a miniature of Bob's own full-size reproduction 1952 Columbia pedal cruiser.*
Below: *Though he had little carpentry experience, Bob built the stair banister.*

Above and left: Single-drawer table and Shaker stand, Crate and Barrel

Because this is a vacation cottage, it's been decorated for comfort rather than luxury.
"We come to the island to relax. Housework is minimized," Barbara says. It's a place where summer's promise is always
present in model ships and Bob's treasured photo of socko New York Yankees Maris, Berra, and Mantle.

PEDAL PUSHERS

saw it. Then I discovered the beaches and I never wanted to leave. We're very fortunate to have a home here."

To keep island life as simple as possible, the cottage has a no-frills layout. The main floor is a single open room—from French doors at the front to a rear door—accommodating the living room, dining area, and kitchen. A modest-size bathroom is tucked behind the staircase on the same level. Above the kitchen is a loft bedroom.

Building on the island can be expensive, but Bob and Barbara saved strain on their budget by purchasing the home's shell from a mainland company. Walls and roof parts were readied in a Newton, Massachusetts, shop, ferried to the island, and assembled in a week on a 16 × 28-foot foundation. With the help of a friend, Bob finished the project, which included such tasks as laying floors and painting.

"I couldn't be happier with the results," Bob says. "For just the two of us, it's perfect. Sweep it out and it's clean. And we're a short bike ride from the water. What better place to be?" □

Above: Delft blue kitchen window tiles from Holland add a touch of elegance. Right: To stay within budget, Bob chose pine for floors, fir for stair railing, and poplar for the kitchen counter. Below: Hang your hat along this bedroom wall where steep roof pitch causes the ceiling to sweep low. Fortunately, there's plenty of headroom around the bed.

Bench above: Crate and Barrel

A GATHERING PLACE

Depending on the season, blackberries, antiques, or good times with friends are harvested here.

A fter 20 years of faithful service rejuvenating its owners' spirits with a soothing, get-away-from-it-all atmosphere, the circa-1840 New Hampshire farmhouse of Estelle Bond Guralnick finally got its hard-earned payback this year. A facelift—performed mainly with skylights, fresh paint, and lighthearted fabrics—returned a crispness to edges that had gone limp from many decades of loving use as a weekend vacation house.

Estelle, a *Country Home*® regional editor from Boston, originally had avoided a decorated look, wanting the house to be "as low-key as possible," she says.

"It was strictly a family hideaway, and I viewed the house as an excuse to go antiquing and indulge my emerging penchant for the whimsical, the offbeat—even the eccentric—in old things."

Top *and* left: *Estelle Bond Guralnick, a* Country Home *regional editor, relaxes in the antique New Hampshire farmhouse that serves as an escape from her home in Boston, two hours away. Kick-back activities mean anything from plopping down on the sofa for a Saturday read to harvesting wild blackberries or just hanging out on the hammock,* above.

BY CANDACE ORD MANROE

Photographs: Interiors, Judith Watts; exteriors, Julie Maris/Semel
Produced in cooperation with WestPoint Pepperell and designer Stanley Hura.

Estelle's "big room" is an invigorating blend of the upbeat and unlikely—from a new chenille slipcover over an old chair from her aunt to sheets used to cover the table, pillows, wing chair, and ottoman. Refinishing the old brown floor with a decorative paint pattern breathed new life into the space.

A GATHERING PLACE

An easy two-hour drive from Boston, the house is located in a peaceful village with only a town hall, general store, and well-stocked library in its center. But nearby there's a lake for swimming, brooks for fishing, tennis courts, and, of course, countless auctions, flea markets, and antiques shows. In the winter, there's cross-country and downhill skiing. "Definitely a house for all seasons," Estelle says.

As the years rolled by, the rooms, tabletops, and even some windowsills slowly filled with treasures culled from hours of lazy snooping on the antiques trail. "I made my purchases gradually," Estelle recalls, "not with the idea of designing a room, but strictly on the basis of what pleased the eye and delighted the mind."

The house became a personal retreat, undemanding, yet restorative to the soul.

Its charm endured—for friends, for Estelle's three grown children, for all but Estelle. Instead of relaxing with a good book, she'd spend weekends there daydreaming about brightening the place with skylights and painted floors. "All the design devices I'd been subconsciously assimilating in my years of styling other people's homes for photography had finally taken their toll," she admits. "I realized that

Above: *Ready-made sheets freshen existing furniture, including the table and wing chair, slipcovered in a striped sheet used both vertically and horizontally.*
Below: *Thought to be a turn-of-the-century addition based on its pressed-tin ceiling, the living room includes an antique iron daybed wrapped in a comforter and topped with pillows covered in sheeting.*

A GATHERING PLACE

though I loved my little old farmhouse, I also felt an insistent urge to give it a lift."

Happily, in this case, a lift did not mean a clean sweep. Estelle chose to preserve the retreat's unique personality, while adding some sparkle. Antiques were to remain in place but freshened, when appropriate, with upholstery. "I finally decided to stop procrastinating and put some ideas into action," she says.

Top of the list was her desire for a decoratively painted floor in what she calls the "big room." The dullness of the old prefinished brown oak boards is now replaced by a classical, oatmeal-colored grid over newly sanded bare wood. Each of the squares is large—24 inches.

Skylights, another priority, now open up the house and act as a crisp counterpoint to the old exposed beams in the big room and kitchen.

In keeping with the low-maintenance aim of a vacation house, ready-made sheets chosen by designer Stanley Hura mix with other fabrics to give a fresh look to existing furnishings. Cheery stripes, polka dots, and checks meld in the big room with a more neutral ticking selected for the sofa. For sheer fun,

Right: *Brightened with skylights, the dining area includes a new Maine-made table and flea-market chairs softened with sheet-covered cushions. "Party Hats" was painted by Estelle's daughter, Aspen artist Jody Guralnick.*
Below: *Splatter-patterned sheets update the kitchen.*
Above: *Embroidery art tops an old store case that came with the house.*

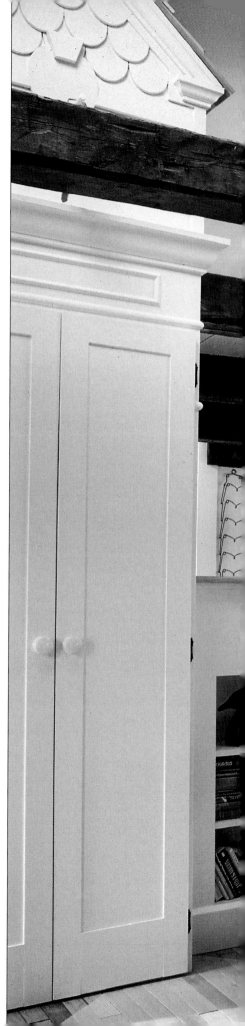

Skylights: Velux-America, Inc. Paint throughout: Benjamin Moore & Co. Fabrics: Waverly

Estelle used a chenille slipcover to update a chair that had belonged to her aunt. In the same upbeat spirit, she added the glow of yellow to the room with the sunflower pillow and the star and moon design on the footstools.

While the changes gave the house a new look, the redo subtly changed Estelle's outlook, too. For the first time since her husband's death five years before, she found herself dashing up to the house on her own to check on the project.

"It was a real bonding process for me," she says. "My husband, Gene, was an avid trout fisherman, and this had been our special retreat. Now it's more of a place to be shared with friends and family. In any case, it definitely feels like home again."

These days, the vintage farmhouse is the preferred destination whenever there's a need to decompress from a busy work week. It's the place to head when the sunny days of summer promise swimming and tennis, or more leisurely pursuits such as antiquing, berrypicking, or just stretching out on the hammock in the shade of the old apple trees.

"Having a vacation house is like being out of school," says Estelle. "I can dip into a book on a Saturday afternoon without a twinge of conscience. It's a license to relax." □

A GATHERING PLACE

Left: *A country French feel pervades this bedroom with its Impressionist-flavored sheets, which are even used at the windows. A quilt made by Estelle's grandmother graces the iron bed.*
Top: *For flair, six different sheet patterns coordinate on a bed. "Party Invitations" is by daughter Jody.*
Below: *The curtains are actually sheets pinned to wooden rings hung on rods.*

STYLE IN·STONE

An 1870s fieldstone home in Bucks County, Pennsylvania,
packs the magnetic power of a lodestone after
a redo for Country Home® *by three top designers.*

Neighboring farmhouses were more plain than fancy, so the Gothic Revival stood out from its peers in the 1870s · Like outspread arms, its circle drive invited company. Inside, a circular staircase made a sweeping statement of domestic well-being and established good taste. Even the facade was dressed stone, not rubble.

BY CANDACE ORD MANROE
PRODUCED BY JOSEPH BOEHM

This gracious old home received great country style from (from left) Tom Cook,
Armstrong; Raymond Waites, Gear; and Joseph Boehm, Country Home.

Floors from Armstrong World Industries, Inc.
Fabrics, wallcoverings, home fashion products: Gear brand

STYLE
IN·STONE

In the early 1930s, a majestic Greek Revival portico was added by then-homeowner Moses Ely—supposedly as a birthday gift for his wife, who admired Southern plantations. Ely worked for the state of Pennsylvania and had salvaged the portico when a historic building in Harrisburg

(the capital) was demolished.

Its refined facade notwithstanding, the farmhouse still managed to lose some of its luster over the years.

As times got hard, the original 90-odd acres were whittled down to just more than 2, and the home was divvied up into three apartments for boarders. Simple survival preempted attention to appearances and forced the removal of both the circular staircase—to make room for boarders—and the circle drive, which probably demanded too much upkeep.

By the time *Country Home* magazine was introduced to the house in 1991, however, it already was well into an upward spiral, with its floor plan brought back to single-family status and

---

Right: *Reversible linen living room draperies are folded back for depth.*
Top: *The dining room heralds a country style that's increasingly sophisticated.*
Above: *Rose, linen, and blue vinyl squares create an inlaid look for the floor.*

Photographs: William N. Hopkins, Hopkins Associates

STYLE
IN·STONE

architectural improvements, including a new kitchen, in place. All that was needed to return the home to its original state of grace was a strong statement of style.

Teaming up with *Country Home* designer Joseph Boehm for the task were two other interior designers: Raymond Waites, Gear design director who sometimes is known as the "father of American country," and Tom Cook, interior design director of Armstrong World Industries, Inc.

"When I first saw the house, it spoke to me of one of the most important looks to which country design is moving—the more refined country look," says Raymond. "The home is at once a classic Pennsylvania stone farmhouse, but with a more refined quality, as shown by the

portico. It was this tension between diverse elements that excited me, because it symbolizes what I'm trying to do with interiors and products."

To get started, the three designers walked through the property. The expected sparring over ideas never materialized.

Left: *The pattern from the kitchen's striated wallpaper is repeated in paintwork on the cabinetry and even on the appliances.*
A jelly cupboard, top, and potting area, above, warm up the kitchen.

STYLE
IN · STONE

"We went in with an open mind," says Tom, "and allowed the house to speak to us. The rooms dictated certain things that we all agreed upon."

The designers knew going into the project that, for the floors, they would use a creative combination of vinyl tiles and resilient flooring.

"We chose patterns that look like traditional American textiles—checked floors, for example, on which we could vary the scale of the checks," Tom says. "In the foyer, we created a small inset 'rug' out of tile."

Another given was attention to warmth and detail. "We insisted the decorating express character through details," says Joseph. "It's the little touches—the jars that go on the jelly cupboard or the flowers at the bedside—that convey real warmth," he says.

"With its classic country style that suggests good breeding and longevity," says Raymond, "I believe this collaborative effort really points to the future—to the more elegant end of country design for our homes." □

Above: *A rose palette, gingham, and christening gowns impart softness.*
Left: *Faux-paint wallpaper and checkerboard-pattern tiles tell the color story.*

August

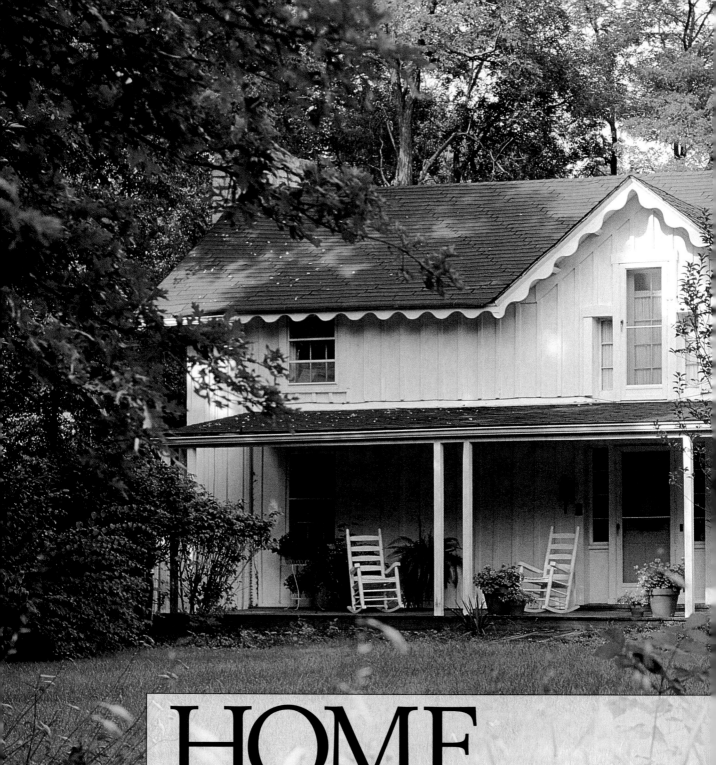

HOME
WITH ALL THE TRIMMINGS

Once their three daughters branched off on their own, Jeanie and Jim Benson moved to Glendale, Missouri, where Jeanie finds creative expression in stenciling decorative designs of the past onto the walls of their historic farmhouse.

By Lisa C. Jones. Produced by Mary Anne Thomson

ALL THE TRIMMINGS

O nly after their three daughters left for colleges and careers could St. Louisian Jeanie Benson convince her husband, Jim, that it was time to look for a smaller house.

But it wasn't easy. Initially, Jim resisted. "How could we leave a home with so many memories?" he argued, remembering the girls' laughter and pitter-patter in the house, the sticky tugs-of-war over saltwater taffy, and the time he and their daughter Beckie planted a tree in the front yard. Jeanie assured Jim that periodical checks on the tree would suffice, so he agreed.

"We decided that the next house would have to be *perfect*," Jeanie says. "We weren't going to leave our other house for just anything."

The house they found is set back from the road and far away from the brick colonials dotting the St. Louis suburb of Glendale, Missouri. Framed by rich foliage and trees, their two-bedroom house is anything but ordinary.

Over the years their home has evolved from two 19th-century log cabins joined by an open-air dogtrot (now the foyer). By 1850, the two cabins were covered with vertical

Above: *Jeanie's steady arm and determination paid off in this hallway embellished with early-19th-century stencil designs.*
Left: *A colorful reproduction Moses Eaton swag and tassel stencil waltzes along the walls amid the vintage furnishings in the living room.*

Photographs: William N. Hopkins, Hopkins Associates   113

ALL THE TRIMMINGS

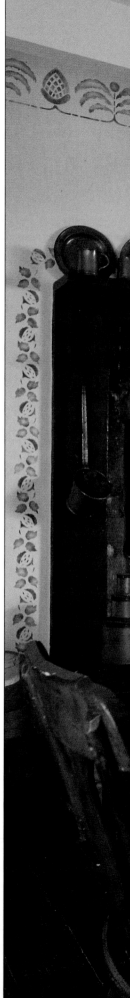

Left: *The timbers of one of the original log cabins form a rugged backdrop for antiques, such as this star-punched pie safe, in the dining room.*
Right: *Soft-hued stencil designs frame the windows in the dining room, which is filled with centuries-old pewter, still lifes, and rustic furnishings.*
Below: *Jeanie's love for blue and white finds expression in the kitchen.*

board-and-batten siding and ornate gingerbread detailing. A summer kitchen and attached garage were added, and the cabins have become less distinct, encompassing a living room, dining room, the master bedroom, and another bedding area.

"It was love at first sight for us," Jeanie says of the home, which has taken almost two centuries to acquire its seasoned form. "We don't mind a few cracks in the plaster or sloping floors; they go with the territory."

Although grateful for their home's rugged nature, the Bensons had experts peel away layers of brittle wallpaper from the coarse, plastered walls, then recoat them with smooth layers of plaster. Eventually, Jeanie turned the walls of their home into canvases of the past—trimmed and garnished with stenciling.

It's no surprise that, fascinated by genteel 19th-century architecture and artistry, Jeanie wanted to put her expertise to good use in this 1800s home, built during the first flush of America's romance with stenciling.

Jeanie's interest in stenciling began 15 years before they moved to the log home. At that time, few stencil suppliers were in their area.

It was serendipity that the Bensons then

met Adele Bishop, founder of a precut stencil company in North Carolina, during a visit to Vermont. Adele introduced Jeanie to a variety of stencil tools, designs, and seminars.

A few years later, Jeanie began selling supplies from her home and eventually from her shop, Jeanie Benson Decorating Arts Center, which specializes in custom-designed and reproduction antique stencils.

ALL THE TRIMMINGS

Jeanie leaves her artistic mark at home, too. Over a 20-day period, she spent more than a hundred hours priming and stenciling the walls of their home.

The colors, soft as a whisper, bespeak a gossamer touch, spiraling up the stairway, traipsing along the living room walls, and encircling the fireplaces and bedrooms.

Many of Jeanie's stencil designs stem from the past where homes along the colonial frontier became galleries for the work of itinerant stencilers, such as Moses Eaton. (His originals are still on display at the Shelburne Museum in Vermont.) She adapted some of Eaton's designs to embellish their home.

The Bensons, both Missouri natives, also enjoy antiques. Shortly after they married more than 30 years ago, the couple purchased some Danish modern chairs, tables, and a sofa, but before the meager pieces required a dusting, a friend convinced them to exchange their furniture for antiques.

Now their history-laden log home brims with reminders of the frontier: the glow of pewter above the hearth, stoneware pails against log walls, and the timeless, sweet grace of stenciling. □

Above: *A sprinkling of fanciful antique baskets adds a delightful charm to the inviting breakfast area with its brilliant southern exposure.*
Left: *"We live here,"* Jeanie says of the *family room that was once a garage. "We wanted something comfortable where we could crash at the end of the day."*

TWICE AS NICE

Janet and Mark Lohman combine talents to get double pleasure from domestic life—she uses her professional skills to decorate their home, he uses his to photograph it, and together with their twin sons, they keep life creative.

Curb appeal sold the couple on the clean-cut, all-American home before they stepped a foot inside its door.

"It looked like all the homes you see all across the country that everybody grew up in," says Janet Lohman. For their first house, she and her husband, Mark, wanted that kind of familiar, wholesome character and its attendant sense of security and stability. The older residence that won their hearts is in Hancock Park, one of Los Angeles's oldest neighborhoods, but it could be Anywhere, USA.

Once inside, the couple was delighted to have their first impressions confirmed. "The traditional floor plan reminded me of the house I personally grew up in," says Janet, "with a center hall that's great for entertaining and a convenient back staircase leading to the kitchen."

It only seems appropriate that the house, built in 1926, had served as a church parsonage before the Lohmans bought it. What's more, the battened-hatches character of the home wasn't just an image but a reality: After moving in, the Lohmans discovered that all the downstairs windows were nailed shut. "The old sashes were broken, and instead of repairing them, the previous owners had just nailed them closed," says Janet.

Other signs of aging demanded prompt attention, but if anyone was qualified for turning the house around, it was the Lohmans. Janet is an interior designer, and Mark is an architectural photographer. In tandem, the couple focused their professional eyes on restoring the house to its original appearance and eliminating '50s-era improvements such as louvered windows and wall-to-wall carpeting.

"We refinished the hardwood floors," says Mark, "and in the living room, replaced a contemporary marble fireplace with a more traditional mantel in keeping with the home's age and architecture."

BY CANDACE ORD MANROE

Top: *The grace and dignity of this Los Angeles home's exterior sold Mark and Janet Lohman,* above, *and their twin sons, Taylor (left) and Parker.* Opposite: *Decor is English country.*

119

Above: *Floral chintzes capture the cheery essence of country English style in the living room, made cozy with sisal rugs and an antique pine coffee table and milking stool.*
Right: *Collectibles include Staffordshire.*

Top right: *A Duncan Phyfe dining table found at a charity sale is flanked by chairs recycled from a local restaurant and slipcovered in $1-per-yard fabric. A chintz pattern connects the living and dining rooms.*

In designing the home's decor, Janet also looked to the architecture for her cues. "In all my work, it's always of first and foremost importance to me to marry the inside of a home with the outside. The architecture dictates the design," she explains.

Although Janet was experienced in creating time-honored designs for her clients who enjoy living with antiques, she had favored, till now, a more contemporary style for herself and Mark. The traditional architecture of the Lohmans' new home, however, required a change of approach for them.

"We had been living in a townhouse, which was contemporary—all beige and hunter green—so I welcomed the opportunity to try something different," she explains.

A mix of comfortable antiques— many picked up at secondhand sales and some family pieces—was in order to underscore the structure's venerable, homey feel. The unassuming but stately architecture required a similar balancing act from those elements selected to decorate its interiors. Fabrics, for example,

had to have flair without being too formal or formidable.

"I had always been attracted to English and French florals," says Janet, "even when they weren't in vogue. They're welcoming, not intimidating, and make a home feel like it's spring year-round."

When Janet and Mark moved into the house, they had no idea children soon would be on the way. In decorating only for Mark and herself, therefore, Janet didn't stop to consider the wear and tear the fabrics and furniture would be required to endure at the hands of two active boys.

"Because we didn't have children when I was decorating, I didn't worry about these things," Janet says. "Then we had the twins and immediately filled up the place." Even so, the English country style she had chosen as a natural complement for the home's architecture proved hardy and fit.

As it turned out, Janet probably couldn't have made a sounder selection. Despite their sophisticated appearance, the country chintzes that play a major role in the home's design are inherently resilient.

Left: *In the den/garden room, Janet covered a thrift-shop chair in an inexpensive pink and white fabric and trimmed it with tassel and twist cording for a high-style effect that belies the affordable cost.* Right: *Bringing warm color and robust country character to the breakfast room with its collection of Quimper (French) and Italian plates, a Welsh dresser was the couple's first antique purchased after marriage. Janet describes the chairs and pine table as "indestructible for two growing boys."*

"By definition, chintz is glazed, so spills from the boys wipe right up. And chintz never really wears out. The only time people replace it is when they're ready for a visual change," says Janet.

With bright, upbeat chintzes repeated at the windows and on upholstered furnishings, the country English design was set in motion. Janet completed the palette by painting the walls of the main living areas yellow—a quintessential country English color. "I was striving for a look that was comfortable and casual. These colors were sunny, welcoming, and young," she says.

Another trait of country English style—an ample quantity of furniture—required no sacrifice from the owners. "We like to entertain

and wanted a living room with a lot of furniture so we could seat many people at one time," says Janet. "We frequently host buffets, and we wanted furniture that was 'user friendly'—that would allow our guests to put their plates and glasses on the tables without worry."

That criteria freed her to acquire furnishings from a variety of sources. The small sofa in the living room dates to the couple's previous contemporary residence, where it was covered in hand-painted canvas. The living room's blue and white chairs came from Mark's mother, who had used them covered in a bright orange contemporary fabric, sans skirts, but with casters.

"I'm also not afraid to go to thrift shops or charity sales. Between

123

TWICE AS NICE

Right: *Janet repeated the master bedroom's country French wallcovering on a headboard of her own design. Antique quilts and quilt pillows reinforce the warm ambience created by the antique round table and bench.*
Left: *Bright colors compensate for minimal light in the boys' room.*
Below: *Nursery furnishings are simple and white to permit toys to make the statement.*

children and earthquakes, things go tumbling," says Janet, explaining her easy-going attitude.

If English country is anything, it is accessories. Here, too, Janet had no problem aligning her own natural propensities with this design dictate. "Because I shop for other people for a living, I love to buy things and sell them later," she says. "The hardest part of decorating for myself is editing down. I like a wide range of accessories, whether it's Staffordshire dogs or glass bowls."

Decorating is never static for Janet; her home is constantly subject to change. One of the bonuses of being married to Mark, she says, is that he can document her designs before a new whim overtakes her. "I drag him around and force him to take pictures. It's great because we're both in creative businesses."

Despite its high country style, the

Lohman home is anything but hands off—even when it comes to the twins. "I never put anything away after they were born," says Janet. "I thought if they learned early on this is how it is, I wouldn't have to go following them around at other people's homes. And it worked." □

Furnished entirely in late-18th-century country antiques compatible with the vintage architecture, the Angiers' Cape Cod house is ideal for showcasing their period-style stenciling, such as the theorem painting above the living room mantel.

Photographs: William N. Hopkins, Hopkins Associates

Right: Each fireboard designed by the couple is based on period motifs.

'CROSS THEIR HEARTHS

Hope and Fred Angier ply the 18th-century craft of fireboard painting from their circa-1780 Cape Cod house in Maine's historic Sheepscot River Valley.

Like a set of nesting tables, the facets of Hope and Fred Angier's lifestyle—their location, home, and work—fit snugly together, each area blending imperceptibly into the others. All are unified by a recurring theme of 18th-century America.

Having restored two historic homes, Fred and Hope knew exactly what they wanted their next residence to be: an antique Cape Cod house dating to the late 1700s that they could bring back to period authenticity. Their criteria for a site were equally specific: The property must have a place in history as well

as a secluded, unspoiled beauty far from the traffic in tourist-driven coastal Maine—a challenge, if not a contradiction in terms. Getting the right historical flavor in their house and site was especially important, for here, Hope and Fred would be creating their 18th-century-style fireboards and theorem paintings. A period atmosphere, they knew, would provide the right inspiration.

With a half mile of the Sheepscot River at its flanks, the 100-acre tract inhabited only by moose, eagles,

BY CANDACE ORD MANROE

Right: Rhodesian Ridgebacks join the Angiers for a respite at the pond.

Above: *The owners moved the antique Cape Cod house to the site and restored it.*

127

'CROSS THEIR HEARTHS

ermine, fox, and deer seemed perfect. The nearest town was Wiscasset, the nearest village Sheepscot, and nary a handprint of man marred the natural vistas. The property's alluvial soil had produced prime forestry during colonial days, when the oldest trees were marked and reserved as "king's timber" for King George. And in the next century, timber used to construct the masts for the ship, Old Ironsides, was felled near the site and floated down the river (which is still populated by indigenous salmon). The property handsomely met each of the Angiers' terms but one: It had no house.

Yet even this posed no real problem. Fred and Hope's commitment to fulfilling dreams not

abandoning them guided the couple to buy the land anyway, trusting that finding and moving in the right house would follow. And they did.

Just five miles down the road was a circa-1780 Cape Cod house. "It had been abandoned for ten years," says Fred. "Even better, it had never had plumbing or wiring so the original structure had not been altered."

Sticklers for authenticity, the couple bought two more structures from the same period—one to use for a kitchen addition and another for spare parts.

"We had the main house dismantled with all of its timbers numbered so we could reconstruct it exactly as it had been when it was first built," says Hope. "Where it was missing trimwork, we used pieces from the other house." They also researched period homes, incorporating features such as feathered sheathing and tiered baseboards (two or three deep baseboards of varying heights stacked one atop the other).

"As we were putting up the original frame, we found rotten rafters on the second floor," says Fred. "We had a portable sawmill brought in and used trees from the property to mill new rafters. Hope, a carpenter, and I did all the work, using mortise-and-tenon and wood-peg construction."

The carpenter was Eric Ekholm, a preservation expert who had worked on restoration of the Mayflower. "We apprenticed ourselves to him," says

Left: *Hope stencils a marine fireboard.*
Top left: *Her work includes chinoiserie.*

Joining the period country furnishings in the Angiers' dining room are some fine examples of Hope's handiwork: decorative stenciling on the walls near the ceiling and wainscoting and a small colonial flag fireboard hung as art.

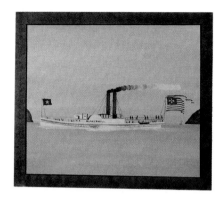

'CROSS THEIR HEARTHS

Fred, "doing everything except plumbing, wiring, heating, and masonry work."

Because the home was rebuilt exactly as it had been in the 1700s, it has a unique, idiosyncratic character, replete with its original imperfections. "We liked all the dips and sags and didn't change them," says Hope. "We wanted the character throughout the home to be homogeneously old, not compromised."

The same resolute integrity guides the couple's early-American-style decorative arts business, Sheepscot Stenciling, which evolved out of their interest in home restoration work.

"I had an artistic desire but no knowledge or training until I met Fred's mother," recalls Hope, who learned stenciling and theorem painting from Elizabeth Chase Angier. Elizabeth had assisted Boston's Esther Stevens Brazier in the 1930s with her efforts to keep alive America's vanishing 18th-century decorative arts, such as theorem painting, reverse-glass painting, and freehand bronzing.

When Hope and Fred began their own restoration business in 1981, they found a ready market for Hope's new stenciling skills.

"After homeowners had beautifully restored rooms," says Hope, "they asked us about accessories appropriate for the period. That's when we started offering theorem paintings. From there came fireboards."

These days, handpainted reproduction fireboards constitute the bulk of their mail-order business. The couple's research reveals that fireboards were in use by 1734 in Williamsburg and were employed even earlier in France. "The original function was to keep birds from coming down the chimney and also to provide an aesthetic block," says Hope. Early construction methods included painting directly onto wood, over wallpaper, or on canvas stretched over a wood frame. "We've adapted the last technique, painting on canvas stretched over solid wood,

for rugged durability," she says.

The fireboards' designs are based on period murals and folk art, thoroughly researched by Fred and Hope. Each one involves several different techniques: color washing, sponging, ragging, faux graining, stenciling, and freehand detailing. The boards' protective varnish includes an additive that suggests a mellow, aged patina.

Throughout the process, Fred and Hope work as a team: He prepares the boards for Hope, who uses her artistry to create the designs. After she's done, Fred adds a faux-grained border that serves as a picture frame. But when it comes to crediting talent, he points to Hope.

"Hope's fireboards and theorem paintings are unique for their depth and richness of color," Fred says. "This is what elicits such a positive response to her work [from the public]," he explains.

Some of their work features the oriental-style decorative paint techniques of chinoiserie and japanning, both of which were popular in early America. Their most unusual offerings are what they call "primoiseries"—chinoiseries with a primitive touch, which they show in the Frank J. Miele Gallery in New York City.

In their antique house, Hope and Fred's fireboards span the hearths in a perfect stylistic fit with their period antiques. The fireboards, in fact, are directly responsible for some of those antiques. "We've been collecting throughout our twenty-two years of marriage," says Hope, "but we've also obtained some of our pieces on the barter system, trading stenciling work for antiques."

There's nothing left to chance in the Angiers' decorating; its success is a result of a carefully shaped master plan. "When we were first married, our home was eclectic, but we developed a plan for getting it homogeneous," Hope says. "You can't do it all at once, but with a plan, you eventually will have the desired theme running throughout your home"—and your life. □

Left: Fred faux-grains a frame around a finished nautical fireboard.

October

Nature doth thus kindly heal every wound.
—HENRY DAVID THOREAU
MARCH 23, 1842

GREAT AMERICAN
VISTAS
GREAT REGIONAL
STYLES

FROM NEW ENGLAND'S CRAGGY GRANITE COASTLINE VEILED
IN A THIN PEWTER MIST TO THE SPUTTERING
SURF ALONG CALIFORNIA'S SUNNY PROMONTORIES, THE
AMERICAN LANDSCAPE IS A HORN OF PLENTY.
EACH REGION FREELY BESTOWS UPON US THE UNIQUE FACE
OF ITS LAND, SOOTHING THE DAILY WOUNDS OF OUR
HIGH-TECH LIVES. LIKE NATURE, COUNTRY DESIGN COMFORTS
AND COCOONS. IT ALSO IS ESSENTIALLY EARTHY,
BRINGING NATURE'S HEALING PROPERTIES INSIDE THE HOME.
JOURNEY WITH US TO SIX REGIONS OF AMERICA
WHERE LOCAL DESIGNERS CREATE SIX DISTINCT EXPRESSIONS
OF COUNTRY THAT ARE INDELIBLY LINKED TO THE LAND.

BY CANDACE ORD MANROE

VISTAS
YANKEE
LANDING

In endless variations on a theme
The waves come in and lace the rocky shore:
One after one long ripples rise and spread
Until they break in necklaces of foam
Or fountain up in a spume, an endless store—
The gentle sea is singing in my head. . . .

—MAY SARTON, "SEASCAPE"
LETTERS FROM MAINE

Near left: *Designer Pat Payne brings seaboard flavor to her family room,* far left, *with Boston nautical antiques, including two yacht binnacles with compasses (on the table and stand). An early trundle bench, pine table, and spool-filled New England bowl join new wing chairs.*
Below left: *Rugged shingles dress the century-old house.*
Preceding page: *An 1800s three-masted sailing vessel model declares regional style on an early-1800s desk.*

Cherry wing chairs: Harden Furniture Co. Country Inns collection. Marine antiques: Brass 'N Bounty. Desk lamp on preceding page: Chapman Manufacturing Co.

Produced by Estelle Bond Guralnick, Joseph Boehm, and Peggy Fisher. Interior photography throughout, except as noted: William N. Hopkins, Hopkins Associates. Seascape photograph: David Muench.

VISTAS

Pelted year-round by the Atlantic's salt spray and in winter by its fierce nor'easters, colonists on the New England coast had little choice but to engage in conversation with the sea. That dialogue's result is a native Northeastern decorating and building style that's hardy, maritime-inflected, and still strong today.

To survive, the first Yankees had to devise ways to not only commune but also contend with the often violent voice of the sea. Their homes quickly became studies in survival, sporting shingle facades that could absorb salt stings with hardly a wince and expanses of small, multilight windows that permitted a full viewing of the sometimes placid, sometimes tumultuous object of their love/hate.

"Living here, it's impossible to ignore the ocean," says designer Pat Payne, an American Society of Interior Designers member, whose Marblehead, Massachusetts, house overlooks the Atlantic.

Northeastern seaboard style means nautical collectibles—brass compasses, telescopes, and captain's desks (see photo inset on preceding page). To Pat, her region's best country style also means the continuation of a certain ruggedness that was implicit in the early days of the nation.

"New England, with its provocative history and culture, triggered my interest in old things," she says. Mixing old primitives with new furnishings is her trademark and "makes for a warm setting that's personal and interesting," Pat explains. She also turns to white for upholstered pieces (the wing chairs) because "it doesn't distract from quilts and antiques, which are central to our region's style."

VISTAS
SOUTHERN SHADE

When I get to be a composer
I'm gonna write me some music about
Daybreak in Alabama
And I'm gonna put the purtiest songs in it
Rising out of the ground like a swamp mist
And falling out of heaven like soft dew.
I'm gonna put some tall tall trees in it...
And red clay earth hands in it
Touching everything with kind fingers
And touching each other natural as dew....

—LANGSTON HUGHES, "DAYBREAK IN ALABAMA"
SELECTED POEMS OF LANGSTON HUGHES

SOUTHERN SHADE

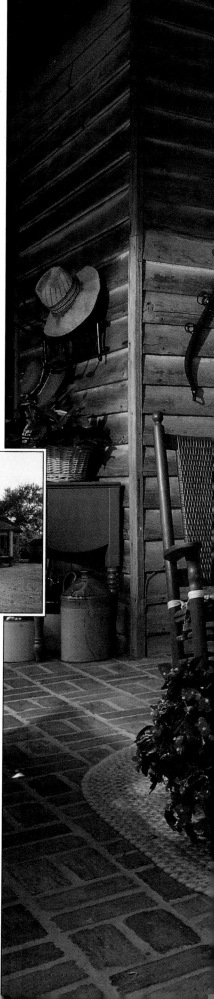

Near right: *Country Home designer and native Southerner Joseph Boehm uses a pair of the region's requisite rocking chairs, cut garden flowers, floral fabrics, and an old braided rug to bring simple Southern charm to the dogtrot-porch,* far right, *of an 1830s La Grange, Georgia, home,* below right. *Preceding page: Old Southern stoneware jugs and one-of-a-kind family accessories decorate a new painted sideboard.*

Beneath a fringed canopy of Spanish moss and ripples of midday heat, the Southern landscape lulls like the gentle sway of a hammock. Sweetened with azalea, jasmine, dogwood, and verbena, the air itself invites a sit-awhile appreciation that is no doubt a wellspring of Southern hospitality.

"The South has a unique relationship to the outdoors," says *Country Home®* interior designer Joseph Boehm, who grew up in New Orleans and spent summers on the Mississippi Gulf Coast. "It has an indoor-outdoor lifestyle that's a combination of sensuality and ceremony. This means an important porch life that cuts across class lines, whether home is a shanty or a plantation. Gathering on the shady porch to relax and commune with family and nature is a way of life."

The dogtrot-porch he designed in a circa-1830 La Grange, Georgia, house illustrates several other aspects of the region's indigenous design style.

"Life in the South is both indulgent and ritualistic," says Joseph. "No good Southern porch is without a comfortable rocking chair, and simple, unpretentious tables are important for our ceremonial iced teas and lemonades. Because Southerners cherish their traditions, true Southern design includes at least a few family pieces."

For the dogtrot-porch, Joe combined a new cricket table and rocking chairs with an older Appalachian twig settee, antique side table, and casual but beloved heirloom accessories. In the lambent dawn or darkening shadows, the space resonates with the spirit of a well-spun Southern yarn.

Cricket table in front of settee, pair of rocking chairs, and painted table on preceding page: Lexington Furniture Industries Weekend Retreat collection. Floral fabric on settee and rocking chairs: Waverly Fabrics

Produced by Joseph Boehm and Peggy Fisher. Landscape photograph: Ed Cooper Photography.

VISTAS

VISTAS
PRAIRIE GOLD

*Everywhere, as far as the eye could reach,
there was nothing but rough, shaggy . . . grass, most
of it as tall as I. . . . As I looked about me
I felt the grass was the country, as the
water is the sea. . . . And there was so much
motion in it; the whole country seemed, somehow,
to be running.*

—WILLA CATHER
MY ANTONIA

PRAIRIE GOLD

Left: *Painter Mark McCormick is at home with heartland style in his 140-year-old Illinois farmhouse, below left.*
Far left: *Midwestern tones in the dining room are set by Mark's paintings of local farm scenes, a prairie palette, and a circa-1830s Illinois chimney cupboard (right) in its original bittersweet and blue paint.*
Preceding page: *Mark's rural landscape crowns an 1870 Illinois dry sink.*

Drapery fabric: Stroheim and Romann, Inc., American collection. Dining table: Thomasville Country Inns and Back Roads collection. Chairs: The Lane Company, Inc., America collection

Produced by Joseph Boehm and Mary Anne Thomson. Landscape photograph: David Muench. House photographs: Barbara Elliot. For more information, turn to Sources.

VISTAS

If Willa Cather's Antonia visited the Midwest today, she would need to engage in some fancy backroads footwork to locate the waving expanses of prairie that so engulfed and awed her nearly a century ago. The great grass seas no longer rage but have receded to rivulets of bluestem or isolated ponds of tall grass, remnants of virgin prairie left after agriculture.

Although the prairie has diminished physically, it still looms large in the mind. And it still influences Midwestern design, just as it did when the rolling grasslands dwarfed even the buffalo. The region's design is a simple farmhouse style that takes its color cues from the prairie, with golden oak floors and furniture as its staples.

Painter Mark McCormick interprets the style with an artist's eye in his circa-1850 farmhouse in St. Jacob, Illinois. "My color sense comes from the area—the colors of nature and the soft, faded colors of antique painted furniture found within a few miles of our home," he says. The hues and textures of the golden plains are strewn about his home—as dried flowers, rush-seat chairs, and antique baskets.

Mark's brand of Midwestern style is scrappy and bold, like the region's settlers. There are no fences in his approach, only horizons. If the right furnishing isn't available, he finds another way: His father built the dining room's corner cupboard, and Mark embellished it with spools and paint. Old quilts and painted pieces—icons of the style—rest within unlikely gallery-spare white walls. Best summarizing the style, though, is Mark's own art: exuberant, fresh, and planted deep in the prairie.

VISTAS
MOUNTAIN MAJESTY

*Far from where we are, air owns those ranches
our trees hardly hear of—open places
braced against cold hills. Mornings, that
new hits the leaves like rain, and we
stop everything time brings, and freeze that one,
open, great, real thing, the world's gift—day.*

—WILLIAM STAFFORD, "MONTANA ECLOGUE"
THE NEW YORKER BOOK OF POEMS

Mountain Majesty

Left: *Designer Lysbeth Manning defines mountain style through the textures of twig and stone and a wildflower palette on pillows.* Far left: *A brilliant rug and shades inject energy into the living room's mountain theme of logs and stone. The soaring, away-from-it-all interior reflects the Colorado home's secluded mountaintop setting,* below left. Preceding page: *Old accessories and wildflowers warm up the hearth.*

Architect: Alpine Log Homes. Contractor: Trends West, Inc. Cocktail table: Hickory Chair Co. Twig chair: Lexington Furniture Industries World of Timberlake collection. Floor lamp: Maitland Smith. Log cabin table lamp: Flynn Devereux. Rocking horse and green box on mantel: Sarreid, Ltd. Timberlake collection. Beacon blanket: Pendleton of Cherry Creek. Wood fruit bowl, bear box, and miniature table and chair: Eron Johnson Antiques

Produced by Mindy Pantiel. Landscape photograph: David Muench. For more information, turn to Sources.

VISTAS

From a perch high atop the Rocky Mountains, life itself seems loftier, transcending the everyday concerns of the world below. The cool, thin air suggests clear thinking, and a dazzling spectrum of wildflowers becomes the day's priority. Towering lodge-pole pines create vertical impulses, drawing humanity a bit closer to heaven— or, at least, to this slice of heaven on earth.

No wonder those who live in the mountain region extract liberally from nature in designing their homes. Cathedral ceilings echo the peaked shapes outside; sweet-scented log walls point to the pine forests that cradled them; fieldstone fireplaces attest to the region's rich mineral reserves.

"Homeowners here are interested in casual living and comfort," says designer Lysbeth Manning, ASID allied member. The country style she created in the living room of a Vail, Colorado, area home fulfills both criteria. "Bright throw pillows bring wildflower colors indoors and set a casual mood. The sofas are eminently comfortable for the relaxing lifestyle people want to enjoy here," she says.

In the mountains, casual comfort is important for sustaining energy. "People here are active. They are avid skiers, snowshoers, and equestrians. Creating a regional style means translating that energy into design," says Lysbeth. In the living room, she imparts dynamism through the vivid floral colors of the rug and Roman shades, and in diverse textures including a rough twig chair and smooth iron-base cocktail table, all cued by nature.

With the region reflected indoors, life becomes integrated, its parts joined like mountain and sky.

VISTAS
NATIVE SUN

*On their right, to the north, stands a mountain shaped like a
flatiron, or like a battleship, with near-vertical walls of volcanic
rock on its horizontal decks, a crenellation of eroded towers,
pinnacles, balanced rocks on pedestals—a voodoo landscape....
Under the evening light, streaming in amber columns
through a mass of clouds, the ancient rock of the mountain takes
on a sullen glow, a mass of mangled iron heated from within
by deep, infernal, other-worldly fire.*

—EDWARD ABBEY
GOOD NEWS

NATIVE SUN

Left: *Designer Jonathan Parks uses textiles such as old Mexican serapes in his 1910 Santa Fe home, below left.* Far left: *Native American influence is strong in his bedroom: A local artist's painting recalls ancient petroglyphs; a late-1800s American Indian cradle board hangs as art; the rag runner recalls native motifs.* Preceding page: *An antique concho belt and old Navaho saddle blanket and rug join an 1890s Midwestern chest.*

Sheets, pillowcases, and bed linens: Utica, J. P. Stevens & Co. Pots, blankets, rugs, chair: Robert F. Nichols. Large pot artisan: Robert Tenerio. Petroglyph painting: Agnes Simms (now deceased)

Produced by Mary Anne Thomson. Landscape photograph: Jeff Gnass.

VISTAS

I n the Southwest, boundaries between the elements blur like rising waves of heat: Fire and earth virtually become one. The baked soil evokes the sun not only in degrees but in color, with its shades of sandstone red and terra-cotta. Not surprisingly, the region's distinctive design style is suffused with these vivid colors of earth and sky.

"Southwestern style is organic," says Santa Fe designer Jonathan Parks. "The unbelievable colors of the area's sunsets, mixed with those of the earth, form an interior palette that's not obstructive to the environment. This gives the feeling of no limits, of being a part of the universe."

Classic adobe architecture borrowed from the Pueblo Indians remains the region's dominant building style. "The neutral [adobe] background allows a blend of textiles, whose colors vary like those in the sunsets or mountains," Jonathan says. Like adobe, textiles are an important element of the style that traces its origins to the region's Native Americans. In his bedroom, Jonathan mixes an old, vegetable-dye Navaho rug with old Pendleton and Beacon blankets and other Native American-influenced textiles, including the sheets.

He rounds out the region's style with collections of Native American pottery, country furnishings, and folk art. Handcrafted in the 1940s, the chair is typical of Southwestern Spanish colonial style, but not every furnishing is local. Jonathan enjoys mixing: A Pennsylvania table houses a prism-art Southwestern lamp. Says Jonathan, the style works when "you feel that everything you own is related to what's happening outside your window."

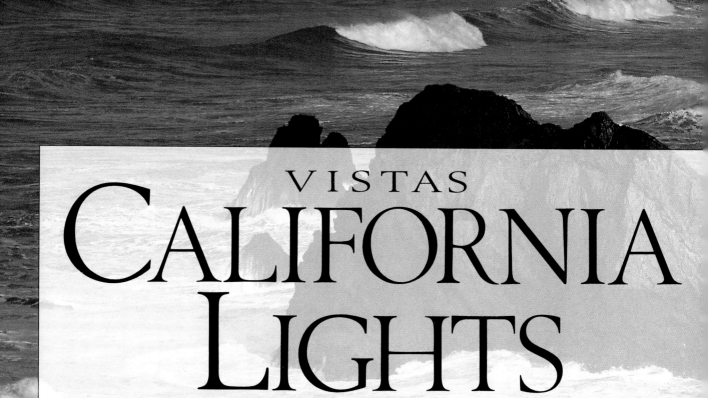

VISTAS
CALIFORNIA
LIGHTS

Facing west from California's shores,
Inquiring, tireless, seeking what is yet unfound,
I . . . look off the shores of my Western sea,
*   the circle almost circled . . .*
Long having wander'd since, round the earth having wander'd,
Now I face home again, very pleas'd and joyous. . . .

—WALT WHITMAN, "FACING WEST FROM CALIFORNIA'S SHORES"
LEAVES OF GRASS

CALIFORNIA LIGHTS

Left *and* below: *Working in an updated 1920s Spanish colonial home, designer Elena Rankin defines California country as an indoor-outdoor style with a Spanish accent. Far left: Elena turned a narrow loggia into a beckoning, outdoorsy space by mixing textures and pulling furnishings close to the arched Spanish windows to soak up sunlight. Preceding page: Two influences on the style, the sea and Spain, join at the entry.*

Iron dining table: Lineage Home Furnishings, Inc. Iron pot stand, glasses, birdcage, garden basket, seashells: Pier 1 Imports. Rug: Berbere Imports. Iron chairs, candelabra, plates: Chilili. Plants: Statice Landscape & Design

Produced with Leslie Gregory. Seascape photograph: David Muench.

VISTAS

Before California garnered a reputation as *the* cutting edge, before Valley girls and Venice Beach rollerbladers, even before Hollywood glitz, the state had a character that was part Spanish mission, part rough-and-tumble West. In defining their region's country style, California designers today are returning to this earlier heritage as a starting point.

"When you think of country style, you think of heritage. Our heritage here has a strong Spanish influence rooted in the era of the ranchos, adobes, and Spanish missions," says designer Elena Rankin, a California native whose loggia design in this Brentwood (Los Angeles area) home serves as a microcosm of the style. "Our regional style is not like Southwestern design because it's less influenced by Native Americans. It's more floral and curved and less geometric," explains Elena.

The early Catholic church is another influence on California country style, which only makes sense given the important role of the Spanish padres and missions in the state's history. Acknowledging this influence of religion in her loggia design, Elena accents with angels.

The style also reflects the rudimentary reality of the early American West. "In the 1800s, life here was rustic," Elena says. "Homes did include finer things from Europe, but ladies would have to wait months for their lace and tapestry to come from overseas. In the meantime, they sat on rustic iron and wooden furnishings."

In the loggia, she included a new iron chaise and table in earth-color finishes, a sophisticated

CALIFORNIA LIGHTS

Right: *A mixture of textures recalling California's old West heritage characterizes this corner still life in which rough iron, wood, wicker, and terra-cotta share space with softer lace and fabric. An antique cupboard houses new pottery and cobalt pieces that echo the blues of the ocean. Live plants inject a sense of the outdoors, another important feature of the region's style. The angel is a reminder of the state's Catholic past,*

Wicker table, blue plate in hutch, lace pillow: Pier 1 Imports. Iron chaise: Lineage Home Furnishings, Inc. Chaise upholstery: Burger Quality Upholstery. Antique hutch: Chilili. Terra-cotta pots: Goodwin International

VISTAS

interpretation of the state's early style. Elena also softened the loggia with some of the European-flavored textiles that would have graced early California homes—tapestry and lace pillows, plus a tapestry throw. "In the early days, textiles would have softened the rougher lines of locally made furnishings," she says.

California's country look may begin with heritage, but from start to finish, it also relates to the land— especially to its radiant, golden light. California rooms are open, with ample windows and glass doors admitting as much natural light as possible. In these indoor spaces, the boundary between the outdoors all but disappears.

"Gardens can feel as if you're inside, and the interior can feel as if you're in the garden," says Elena. "It's appropriate to use the same pieces indoors and outdoors: Terra-cotta pots, iron furniture, and rustic wood pieces work both places. With the expanses of windows in California interiors, even the light is similar indoors and out."

Allowing the light full play, walls and fabrics most often are crisp white, then dappled and given depth by a wash of sunshine pouring through the windows. In addition to serving as a canvas for nature's light show, the white backgrounds suggest another California image—the state's pale, sandy beaches and dunes. Elena adds blue to the mix, recalling the rich cobalt hue of the Pacific Ocean.

With its beach colors bathed in natural light, California country's clean design has more of a contemporary feel than any of the other regions' country looks. But with its roots planted back in time, in the Spanish colonial and Old West eras, this regional style is more timeless than trendy—more classic than au courant. □

Right: *A burst of red, white, and blue patriotism is displayed on the shelf above Mitchell Turner's bed.* Below right: *Nancy Turner shares her front porch with son Mitchell and married daughter Ashley Carroll, who lives nearby with her own family.*

Georgia Peach

Nancy Turner is enjoying the fruit of her labors—a farmhouse in the heart of Georgia graced with a fine collection of American country antiques.

Y*ou are a neighbor with those of the past as well as those of the present. If you walk where they have walked and live where they have lived, you do belong.*
> —Charlotte McCartney
> *Once Upon a Town*, 1985

Nancy Turner had an epiphany when she read McCartney's thoughts about a small Vermont town. The words captured Nancy's feelings about her 130-year-old house.

"That's exactly how I feel about it," says Nancy. "In a way you don't really own an old house. It's yours for a time. But there were others who came before you and others will come after you."

From her first visit, she knew this Marietta, Georgia, farmhouse was for her.

"I was moving back to Georgia after spending some time in Charlotte [North Carolina], and I remember wishing this could be the period in my life when I would find

BY STEVE COOPER. PRODUCED BY RUTH REITER

Georgia Peach

the perfect house," she says, "a dream house I'd been thinking about since I was in college, the one that I could see in my mind's eye. It was this exact house. A simple old country farmhouse behind a white picket fence. It's unpretentious, but with just the right amount of charm."

When she purchased the five-acre property six years ago for herself and her two children, Ashley (who has since married) and Mitchell, the dwelling was in reasonably good working order. But interiors were tired survivors from the 1950s with green shag carpet, worn paint, and gloomy draperies.

Nancy hired contractors to add new heating and air-conditioning systems, cap the house with a cedar shake roof, renovate the attic as a suite for her daughter, insulate wherever possible, open up three small rooms to create a spacious keeping room, and coat walls with fresh paint.

The work revealed every inner secret of her house, and Nancy became intrigued by the question of the structure's age. Her interest peaked when an old Georgia clay brick chimney was exposed by workers tearing into the attic.

"I started talking to some of the older neighbors and found that they believe a one-room dwelling was on the site of my house

Top: *The stairs were added when Ashley's attic suite was built.* Above: *For years before moving into this small white house with a picket fence, Nancy imagined herself living in just such a place.* Left: *Nancy chose light festoons to dress her front windows so she could take full advantage of views toward both Little and Big Kennesaw mountains.*

back around the time of the Civil War," she says.

Nancy surmises that the house grew as the families who lived there grew. New rooms clustered around that single room where it all began.

"There used to be a cotton-growing plantation down the road, and I think this house might have started as a part of that plantation. It's a wonderful location. The house sits on a high knoll and is surrounded by six centennial oak trees. It would be hard to find a better spot to build," she says.

Because the home has a long history, it seems only fitting that it should be filled with antiques. Nancy has cultivated her interiors with a collection of furnishings she has been gathering most of her life.

She describes herself as someone who hunts for bargains. Along the way she has found an unpainted corner cabinet from the late 1800s; hand-hooked rugs from the 1830s; an aging dry sink in which she houses her television; and numerous antique dolls, children's clothes, satchels, and

Above: *When she was still in high school, Nancy paid $7 for the low, long bench now standing in her entry. "Daddy was appalled when I brought it home, but I've had it ever since," she says. The clothing above the bench dates from the mid-1800s.*
Left: *To give the dining room floor a livelier personality, Nancy painted it with red and cream checks. The miniature colonial home sitting atop the pie safe was a birdhouse. When Nancy bought it, some pieces of nest were still inside.*

Georgia Peach

other everyday accessories for youngsters.

"When I was in high school, a friend's mother got me interested in collecting. She was a decorator and the only person I knew who enjoyed collecting things. My friend had an old quilt on her bed and an old pine chest. I loved that look. So by the time I went off to college, I took a braided rug and big, plaid bedspreads. I've never had any style in my home other than American country," says Nancy, who collaborated on her home's decor with Bettye Wagner, owner of a Marietta antiques store managed by Nancy.

As Nancy's tastes have evolved, she has narrowed her special interest to two areas: children's clothing and textiles.

"I love items that are personal. It's funny, because I hate to sew. I'd rather make an adjustment with a safety pin than sew up a shirt. So when I think of every stitch and every seam and all the effort involved in hand sewing, I'm amazed. I appreciate things that are done with so much love," she says.

Among her regrets is that so few pieces remain from her own family's history. One that does stand out as a gem is not an article of clothing. It's a late-1800s pie safe built by Nancy's maternal grandfather.

The safe towers in a corner of Mitchell's room. As a display cabinet, it's home for

Above: A stack of bread plates from Nancy's grandmother sits among the assorted utensils on the kitchen table. Nancy likes the brick kitchen floor: "I love the low maintenance; just sweep it and it's clean. There's not a lot of scrubbing and waxing to do."
Left: Nancy had walls removed from three small rooms to create more open spaces, including this family room. She mixed newer upholstered wing chairs with an antique trunk, a turn-of-the-century hooked rug, and a mid-1800s dry sink.

165

Georgia Peach

Above: *Though this bedroom now accommodates Nancy's guests, it was once the parlor. The fireplace's chimney is original, but the hearth is new.*
Near right: *Beneath the guest bedroom's rope bed is a trundle where a child might have slept.*

toys from bygone years. Here are an old drum, a fielder's mitt, and a long-loved toy pony. Here, too, is a doll from Nancy's father's boyhood.

"The pie safe stood for years on the back porch of my mother's place in Hepzibah, Georgia," says Nancy. "It's very precious to me because so few things have survived from my mother's family."

These various antiques have taken on a quality of friendship for Nancy. They speak in muted voices of a distant, intriguing past.

Nancy says, "I love finding fine old pieces because they connect me to the past and they will continue to bring pleasure into the future." □

December

TOMIE'S CHRISTMAS STORY

Children's book illustrator and author Tomie dePaola adorns his New England home with exuberant whimsy come Christmas.

Tomie dePaola's wry blue eyes crinkle then widen as an image only he can see springs to life from imagination's slumber. Something good, perhaps delicious, is astir in Tomie's mind, and it's turning his entire visage into one of happy animation not unlike the children's book illustrations that have made him famous.

What's animating Tomie might be an idea of a new character to draw, or it might be what he's going to have for dinner. Anyone familiar with his books (*Bonjour, Mr. Satie; Tattie's River Journey;* and *The Quilt Story,* among others) would know at a glance that the ebullience Tomie brings to his art is identical to that which he

Above right: *Tomie dePaola uses candles and folk art to bring holiday cheer to his barn-style New England home,* **right.**

BY CANDACE ORD MANROE
PRODUCED WITH PEGGY FISHER
AND ESTELLE BOND GURALNICK

TOMIE'S STORY

lives by. The same liveliness, tempered when appropriate by a more serious grace, informs all aspects of his life. Tomie may be cajoling friends one minute, somberly listening to classical music the next. Nothing epitomizes these diverse dimensions better than his home—and no season better than Christmas.

Like a good story, Tomie's home has the right setting, resting on the outskirts of New London, Connecticut—one of New England's most picturesque villages of white steeples, snowy lawns, and 200-year-old buildings. Tomie's house isn't old, but it does have a place in history. Built in the 1970s, it's the prototype for Yankee Barn homes—contemporary interpretations of classic New England barn architecture.

Beginning with the lavender exterior paint trim, the abiding mood is exuberant. Festoons of tiny glittering lights and fragrant greens enliven every nook and surface of the house, and mammoth trees are decorated both indoors and out. Petite vases of amaryllis outline the windowsills like a border illustration from one of Tomie's colorful books.

Yet amid all the festivity there runs a more serious undercurrent. Certain rooms or portions of rooms are massed with votive candles and religious folk art in an almost altarlike manner, making silence the most appropriate response.

Left: *Since the 1950s, Tomie has decorated one tree with paper roses, a Middle Ages symbol of Mary.*

Top: *The family room's crisp white walls and barn architecture allow the eye to soar to a votive border.*

Above: *Hearts, a trademark of Tomie's art, also are a favorite collectible.*

TOMIE'S STORY

There's nothing hushed about the big Christmas party at Tomie's, however. Nearly the entire town attends. A tradition for the past 15 years, Tomie's gala is an event most people look forward to all year long—and talk about till the next. (In fact, we learned details about Tomie's last party from waitresses at the restaurant where we stopped our first night in town.)

"I grew up in a very dramatic family, which always had a Christmas Eve party that would last till two or three in the morning," says Tomie, who sees himself as simply continuing his Irish-Italian family's tradition. "It never dawned on me until I was older that my parents' Christmas party was one of the few ways people could celebrate during the war years. Both parents had such a joy of life. I'm not at all sure that's not hereditary."

The social bustle that occurs in his own home during the holidays points to the importance of the season in other areas of Tomie's life. Christmas is a dominant theme in his professional repertoire, and indeed much of his reputation comes from his Christmas books.

It's also a season that Tomie personally holds in quiet awe as a time for contemplating life's mysteries and wonders. That's not surprising, considering that Tomie's background, after art school, included time in a Benedictine monastery—on several occasions.

Left: *Like an altar, the living room mantel, with its religious folk art, evokes a quieter spirit of Christmas.*

Top: *A gourmet cook, Tomie has six ovens (out of view to the left) in his kitchen, all of which are used to prepare holiday foods.*

Above: *Tomie adorned this plate with dried fruits.*

TOMIE'S STORY

"My first time in Weston Priory, I stayed six months," says Tomie. "When I entered again, it was for only six weeks. After that, it was for six weekends. A Baptist friend of mine said, 'Next time, just call it in.'" Tomie's humor ensures against *too* much somberness.

After the monastery, Tomie spent five years creating liturgical art, and he says the Benedictines' enthusiasm for the arts benefited him. But the monastic influence most evident at Christmas is votive candles— a part of every room.

"I knew from the early days that the best place to buy votives was the cathedral store. I was buying so many that the clerk asked if I was a church," Tomie recalls. "She said, 'Well, sir, you're buying more than the cathedral, so I'll give you the church discount anyway.'"

Another important Christmas decoration is Tomie's collection of religious folk art. These pieces inject bold color and warmth into Tomie's pristine, all-white rooms. "Some kids tell me white's not a color. I say, 'Sure it is—I can show you my tube of white paint.' You can never have too much white," he says.

At Christmas, white becomes the perfect canvas for the joyful story Tomie never tires of telling, year after year. □

Editor's note: Look for Tomie's new holiday book, Jingle, the Christmas Clown, *published by G. P. Putnam's Sons.*

Left: *Vases of hyacinth and pots of poinsettias, plus Santas add artistry to Tomie's bedroom.*

Top: *Antiques in their original painted finish brighten a corner of the master bedroom.*

Above: *Religious folk art fills architectural niches.*

WITH A
Rosy Glow

Country Home® *magazine's Ann Maine and her family celebrate the softer side of Christmas amid a pastel palette and favorite family furnishings.*

An Iowa blizzard may be howling at the windows, but inside the Des Moines home of *Country Home* magazine executive editor Ann Omvig Maine the peace and warmth of Christmas rest secure.

Illumined by the comforting flicker of candlelight and a fire at the hearth, the Tudor-style cottage Ann shares with her husband, Mike, and daughter, Emily Manternach, stands as a cozy counterpoint to the bone-chilling world outside.

Physical warmth is only part of the cottage's appeal. The values represented on the pages of *Country Home*—a respect for ethnic heritage (Ann's roots are Scandinavian), family tradition, personal meaning, and creative expression—take tangible form in the Maines' house. And Christmas, more than any other time of year, illustrates just how dramatically Ann's personal and professional lives merge.

"A deep regard for heritage and family has always been an important part of my life, even before I came to *Country Home*," says Ann. "Christmas is the time for expressing our values at home through special decorating, foods, and traditions," she says.

The family's circa-1920 cottage is dressed for the holidays starting around Thanksgiving and continuing until February. Cheery cut greens, herbal wreaths, sparkling white lights, and warm holiday scents wafting from the kitchen create a strong impression of this house as a safe haven—the kind of place you wouldn't mind being in to weather a blustery storm on Christmas Eve.

Blush-painted plaster walls, which change intensity according to the play of light, create a serene ambience that's

By Candace Ord Manroe
Produced by Joseph Boehm And Shelley Caldwell

Left: Country Home *magazine's Ann Maine enjoys Christmas with her husband, Mike, and daughter, Emily Manternach, in their Des Moines, Iowa, cottage,* above. Opposite: *The living room porch-post lamp points to Ann's lifelong interest in collecting: At age 8, despite her dad's protests, she hauled posts from Great-Aunt Crescy's porch. The grain-painted corner cupboard was handed down from Ann's family.*

WITH A
Rosy Glow

underscored by soft lace, muted fabrics, wicker, and painted furnishings.

"We wanted a romantic interior to complement the pseudo-Tudor exterior," says Ann. Through her daily contact with home design on the magazine, she is supplied with ample decorating ideas—and the confidence to implement many of her own.

"New wicker furniture with floral chintzes seemed to mix well with both the family pieces and the painted furnishings I'd picked up over the years," she explains. Plus, new furnishings were more affordable than antiques.

Mike, though also acquainted with home

design through his position as the managing editor of the magazines that comprise *Better Homes and Gardens* Special Interest Publications, is comfortable with Ann acting as the home's primary designer. His role is that of project engineer, implementing Ann's decorating ideas, such as special crackled paint finishes on some of the home's woodwork.

"Sometimes I have trouble envisioning what she's trying to achieve," says Mike, "but I trust her instincts. I haven't been disappointed yet."

Although Ann's heart is in turn-of-the-century or earlier architecture, she found the house's exterior charming and its capacious front window irresistible. "Also, I was attracted to the potential of converting the attic into another bedroom," she explains.

The rose-petal palette, which the couple jokingly

Preceding pages: *Ann's living room coffee table shows Iowa ingenuity— it's a chicken crate she found at a garage sale, then topped with slate and a hooked rug bought at auction for $3.50 during college.*
Opposite: *A circa-1880 wooden chandelier from a Scandinavian church in Minnesota enhances the dining room's romantic look. The sugar bucket beneath the bench was Ann's grandfather's.*
Above: *The painted cupboard is dated 1986, the year of Emily's birth.*
Left: *Collections fill a wood-burned shelf.*

calls "Pepto-Bismol pink," was dictated by the living room's richly tinted wool carpet that covered the hardwood floors when they bought the home.

"The last owners had been in the house fifty years, and they had never remodeled," says Mike. "We had to replace the roof, plumbing, and wiring, so there was little budget left for decorating. We opted to keep the original carpet, which was in good condition, and base our colors around it."

The soft palette made an appropriate backdrop for memorabilia that had been in Ann's family for generations—a hanging corner cupboard, small green table, her grandfather's sugar bucket, and, on the bedroom nightstand, the locket her grandfather presented to her grandmother during their courtship.

"The idea of passing things on is very important to me," says Ann. "I bought a folk-art painted cupboard dated 1986, the year Emily was born, with the idea of it one day becoming hers." In the meantime, Emily's room is graced with a child's wooden rocker that Ann's great-grandparents bought for their baby daughter then handed down.

Not surprisingly, Emily already has a healthy regard for heritage. "One of her favorite comments to me is, 'When you kick the bucket, is this mine?'" says Ann. "I'm working hard to turn her into an antiques collector."

Christmas is an ideal time to indulge a passion for the past—and to start new traditions. The Maines do both. Ornaments Ann has collected over the years are brought down

from the attic and hung on the tree, along with satin ribbons and red wooden beads. "The tree isn't finished until Emily puts the crocheted angel on the top," says Ann.

Nor is the holiday complete without Norwegian codfish and lefse (a flatbread), and about 14 different kinds of Christmas cookies prepared each season by Ann's mother. "I don't have to bake Christmas cookies," says Ann. "My mother makes trays of them using recipes from her mother and her mother-in-law."

More important to the Maines' holiday than food or ornaments, though, is family: "Ultimately, spending time with our families is what Christmas is all about," says Ann. □

Left: Emily's bedroom is a study in family history: The baby dresses and tea set were Ann's; the pegboard is from the 1876 house built by Emily's great-great-great-grandparents; the rocking chair was Emily's great-great-grandmother's; and the cedar chest came from her grandparents' farmhouse.
Above: A locket and lamp from Ann's grandmother warm the master bedroom.

Many Happy RETURNS

It's Christmas once again and time for Tom and Polly Minick to dust off the holiday collections for their sons' homecoming.

BY STEVE COOPER

Polly Minick is a collector of miniature Santas, feather trees, pewter cookie molds, and other joyous holiday treasures. But foremost she is a collector of family Christmas memories.

"All I really want is for our boys to be home at Christmas. Then I'm happy," Polly says.

When she and her husband, Tom, welcome home their three grown sons and a daughter-in-law, the Minicks gather in the same rooms where the sons were once youngsters. The family has lived in the same Ann Arbor, Michigan, house since the early 1960s.

For the holidays, Polly orchestrates the home's cheerful mood, using the distinctive smell of freshly cut pine, the embracing aroma of a kitchen warmed by baking, and the display of an ever-

expanding array of Christmas decorations.

It's all a labor of love for her family's enjoyment.

"There's only been one Christmas when we couldn't all be together," Polly says. "Typically, we have a Christmas Eve celebration here or with our neighbors—but we never open our gifts that night. We save them for a big celebration on Christmas morning."

When the Minick sons—28-year-old twins John and Jeff, and Jim, 27—return for a visit from their homes in California and Michigan, it is to a home that has changed as much as they have through the decades. When the family first moved in, there was plenty of room for wrestling in the three-bedroom, ranch-style house. But by the time the boys reached kindergarten,

rooms already seemed as tight as last year's blue jeans. So walls gave way as a family room was added and the kitchen and dining room were enlarged.

As the boys grew toward their 6-foot-plus teenage size, the house seemed to shrink a notch with each passing year. But when they began leaving home

Far Left: *Filled with greens, Santas, and sleds, this family room addition is the home's gathering place.*
Top: *In front, the Minicks' home looks as it did when it was built in 1963.*
Left: *On Christmas Eve, Tom and Polly Minick were joined by sons John (left) and Jim (in rear). Their other son, Jeff (John's twin), and his wife, Linda, were unable to arrive from California in time for the picture.*

Photographs: William N. Hopkins, Hopkins Associates

Opposite: *Looking past the living room Christmas tree and through the windows, visitors see another gaily lit tree in the gazebo outside.*
Above: *Polly began collecting game boards to decorate walls because she didn't like the look of either paintings or photos.*
Right: *Twenty years ago, Polly bought the small snowman at far right. The tallest was purchased only two years ago.*

for college, snug rooms became spacious again.

"We were getting pretty cramped raising a bunch of athletes," Polly says. "But now, the home is just the right size for Tom and me, so we don't have any plans for leaving. We're a little crowded when everyone is home at Christmas. But it's the kind of crowded that a family enjoys."

As a corporate vice president, Tom could easily afford a newer, larger home for the family.

"But why?" he asks. "We built here to begin with because we like the location. We're in kind of a woodsy setting, but we're

only a few minutes from downtown. And, if we moved, we'd have to give up our neighbors and a great neighborhood."

Should the couple feel like getting away from home, they can always take the hop north to their vacation cabin on Lake Huron's Drummond Island, as they do with their sons for a few days after Christmas each year. (The retreat was featured in the February 1991 issue of *Country Home*® magazine.)

Both houses are decorated with booty from Polly's countless forays to swap meets, antique shops, and garage sales. "I started

Many Happy
RETURNS

Many Happy RETURNS

buying antiques when Tom and I were first married," Polly says. "In those days, antiques weren't such a fashionable interest as they have become. Then it was a matter of necessity to save money."

Polly's first major investment—major, that is, in terms of the family income during that time when Tom was a sheriff's deputy—was Christmas decorations.

"We were married in November, so Christmas came up right away," Polly says. "I went to the dime store and loaded up on all these blue decorations. Nothing I would choose today. But it started me off. Got me thinking in terms of decor and arranging colors."

By the time the boys came along, she was collecting painted furniture pieces, kitchenware, and

pottery. Though she was the buyer, she always looked for ways to involve the whole family in her infectious avocation.

"If we were driving around, I'd encourage them by offering an ice-cream cone to the first one who spotted an antique store," she says. "I found some great shops that I would have missed."

Because the boys were active in sports, the Minicks seemed to spend their school years through college on the road as games took the family all around Michigan. Polly took full advantage of the opportunity to discover new shops.

She particularly recalls the time son Jim helped her spot a pine cupboard while the family was on one of their expeditions to a wrestling tournament.

"He was about nine

Right: *When her sons moved on to college, Polly replaced football posters with quilts.*
Top: *A collection of 15 Noah's arks are among Polly's many prized possessions.*
Above: *Polly hooked the welcome rug.*

Many Happy
RETURNS

then. I saw the piece, loved it, and brought it home," Polly says. "The whole way home, Jim was complaining about riding in the car with that cupboard. Well, it was in this house for fifteen years and now it's up at the island. Jim called the other day and we were talking about his own home. And what do you suppose was the one piece he asked if he could have? That old pine cupboard he once complained about."

As a veteran collector, Polly has become ever more selective through the years in the items she buys and those she lets pass. The fun for her has always been in the hunt as much as in the acquisition.

"You're looking for something, though you really don't expect to find it. Then, suddenly it's in front of you. That

happened to me the other day when I found a miniature, blue Noah's ark that I put out for Christmas. I hadn't seen one in a year and a half, and there it was," she says.

With just such antique finds, Polly has transformed the Minick home from the ordinary to the extraordinary.

"When the family gathers on Christmas to open presents, I want this home to be a special place, and it is," she says.

Tom agrees.

"Polly's the life of this home," he says. "What she does is always kind of a surprise. Obviously, the Christmases we had when the boys were little were quite special. But even now, after all these years, she manages to find a way to make each holiday just a little more memorable than the last." □

Index